HAGOP KEVORKIAN SERIES ON NEAR EASTERN ART
AND CIVILIZATION

The publication of this work has been aided by
a grant from the Hagop Kevorkian Fund.

THE GREAT ARAB CITIES IN THE 16th–18th CENTURIES AN INTRODUCTION

André Raymond

New York University Press • New York *and* London • *1984*

Library of Congress Cataloging in Publication Data

Raymond, André.
The great Arab cities in the 16th–18th centuries.

(Hagop Kevorkian series on Near Eastern art and civilization)
Translated from the French.
"Printed version of four lectures given in April and May 1983 at the Hagop Kevorkian Center at New York University"—Pref.
Bibliography: p.
Includes index.
1. Cities and towns—Arab countries. 2. Arab countries —Social conditions. I. Title. II. Series.
HT147.5.R39 1984 307.7'64'09174927 84-9895
ISBN 0-8147-7391-5 (alk. paper)

Clothbound editions of New York University Press Books are Smyth-sewn and printed on permanent and durable acid-free paper.

Contents

Preface

Except for a few details, this book is the printed version of four lectures given, in April and May 1983, at the Hagop Kevorkian Center at New York University.

I proposed to study the great Arab cities of the Mediterranean world during the Ottoman era, that is to say, between the sixteenth and eighteenth centuries. This delimitation of the period and of the cities under study makes it possible to define a relatively homogeneous ensemble with regard to their size (and thence their urban problems); their geographical, socioeconomic, and cultural features; and their historical evolution. One can therefore expect that urban characteristics common to these different cities can be brought to light. Another advantageous factor is the exceptional wealth of the available archives, which provide virtually inexhaustible sources of documentation. At the same time, in their ancient quarters, the cities themselves offer an abundant repertory of urban forms and monuments that have not yet become totally dilapidated and that retain some coherence.

It was naturally impossible, in the framework of the lectures, to tackle all the problems brought about by the evolution of these cities during three centuries of their history. I have, therefore, confined myself to those aspects of this evolution which I considered to be most significant, focusing mainly on questions of urban structure.

To attempt an exhaustive study would be to come up against great difficulties. For one thing, many badly needed monographs are still lacking. Classical (but often old) studies are available on Fez (Le Tourneau), Algiers (Lespès), Cairo (Clerget and Abu Lughod) and Aleppo (Sauvaget), and quite recently on Ṣanʿā (Lewcock and Serjeant). But a number of important cities, such as Tunis, Damascus, Mosul, and Baghdad, still await "their" book. Furthermore, in the case of the best-studied cities, the modern era has often been treated with all the negligence that was the rule, until fairly recent times, with regard to the Ottoman period.

Paradoxically, the above-mentioned wealth of documentation constitutes an additional problem. The interest taken for some twenty years now in these "new" sources (judicial court and *waqf* documents, governmental Ottoman archives) is bringing about a complete revision of the history of Arab countries in modern times. Numerous important studies are now under way. I was able to use some of them, but many others will be completed only in years to come. By that time, the idea that one may propose of the great Arab cities will have changed markedly.

Thus, one can rightfully consider that attempting such a comprehensive study would be somewhat premature. It seemed to me, however, that, while awaiting the conclusion of the various studies I have just mentioned (one of the most promising of which will, unfortunately, remain unfinished, since Antoine Abdel Nour was killed in Lebanon, in June 1982), it would be useful to suggest a few points of reference and to take stock of some of the problems presented by the great cities that came within the Ottoman sphere of influence during the sixteenth century as provincial capitals of the empire: Algiers, Tunis, Cairo, Damascus, Aleppo, Mosul, and Baghdad.

This work was made possible because of the generous aid afforded by New York University's Hagop Kevorkian Center for Near Eastern Studies, which provided me with the opportunity of giving the lectures from which this book originated. I wish to express particular thanks to Professor Bayly Winder, who first invited me to New York University; to Professor Farhad Kazemi, Director of the Center; and to Ms. Doris Miller, who organized my stay in New York. Assistance from the Centre National de la Recherche Scientifique (the GREPO of Aix-en-Provence, directed by Professor Robert Mantran), from the Direction Générale des Relations Culturelles of the Ministry of Foreign Relations, and from Saint Antony's College at Oxford also contributed much to the progress of my work. Finally, I would like to thank Ms. Camilla Saadoun, who translated the texts, and Mr. Jean Prodhomme, who executed most of the plans illustrating this study.

André Raymond
Aix-en-Provence

Note

The transcription used is basically that of *Arabica.* I have not used the forms *s* or *es* for plurals in the text for transliterated terms (italicized).

At the back of the book I give the plans of the seven towns that form the main subject of the study, toward the end of the eighteenth century, or during the first decades of the nineteenth century, before the beginning of their "modernization" (Ills. 79–85). The town plans were drawn up from various documents: for Algiers, Pelet's plan of 1832, corrected so as to restitute the town center that was destroyed in 1830 and 1831; for Tunis, the map used by J. Revault in his books on Tunis (*Palais et demeures de Tunis,* 1967–1974); for Cairo, the plan of the *Description de l'Egypte* (drawn up, 1798–1801); for Damascus, H. Wulzinger and C. Watzinger's plan (*Damaskus,* 1924); for Aleppo, the topographical map of 1928–1929; for Mosul, the map published by F. Sarre and E. Hertzfeld (*Archäologische Reise,* 1911–1920); for Baghdad, the plan drawn up by J. F. Jones (*Memoirs of the Province of Baghdad,* 1857), a photograph of which I obtained from the British Museum.

In the text, references to the grids of the various maps are given between brackets; the abbreviations AL., T., C., D., A., M., and B. designate the different cities mentioned. The following letter and number indicate the precise location.

Given the enormous differences of surface area of the town studied (e.g., Algiers, approximately 45 hectares; Cairo, more than 700 hectares), it was not possible to apply a common scale to these maps.

The bibliography proposes to provide a general orientation concerning the problems of the cities in modern times; only the more accessible works have been mentioned. It is thus essentially limited to books published in European languages. Of course, many studies in Arabic were also used, and these are mentioned in the notes.

List of Illustrations

Almost all the illustrations are the author's photographs. Sources of the other illustrations are as follows:

Ill. 1: J. Sauvaget, "Esquisse," plans VIII and X

Ills. 2, 14, 21, 39, 56: J. Sauvaget, *Alep,* plans LXII and LXX; fig. 55; plans LXIII, LXVII, LXVIII

Ills. 5, 24, 28, 30: *Description de l'Egypte*

Ill. 9: R. Hay, *Illustrations of Cairo,* fig. 24

Ill. 10: E. W. Lane, *Manners and Customs,* p. 323

Ill. 11: D. Roberts, *Egypt and Nubia*

Ills. 17, 18, 25, 38, 76: P. Coste, *Architecture Arabe,* pls. XLIII, XLIV, XXIII, XLVI, XLI

Ill. 19: F. Aalund, "The wakālat Bazarᶜa," fig. 3
Ill. 23: A. Rīḥāwī, "Ḫānāt," fig. 5
Ill. 31: J. C. David, "Alep," fig. 12
Ill. 35: Duthoit, Photographies des monuments d'Alger, Monuments historiques, no. 51685
Ill. 37: P. Coste, Manuscrit de la Bibliothèque Municipale de Marseille, no. 1308
Ill. 42: Solange Ory
Ills. 48, 52: A. Patricolo, "Compte Rendu," pls. CCVI, CCXI
Ill. 64: E. Prisse d'Avennes, *L'Art Arabe,* pl. XXXIII
Ill. 74: G. Marçais, *L'Architecture Musulmane d'Occident,* fig. 265

CHAPTER ONE

The Ottoman Empire and Arab Cities

1. THE OTTOMAN EMPIRE

1.1. Organization of the Empire

The Ottoman conquest covered nearly all the Arab world during an expansion that required little more than half a century, from 1516 (occupation of Syria by Sultan Salīm) to 1574 (the definite occupation of Tunisia by Sinān Pasha). By the latter date, the empire became stabilized within frontiers that were barely to change until 1830, with the exception of a few peripheral retreats (e.g., Yemen). Around the Arab Mediterranean, only Morocco remained outside the empire. The threats pending on the eastern frontier, where the conflict with Persia continued until the end of the eighteenth century, did not place Ottoman domination in peril. After the conquest by Salīm, in 1516, Mosul did not leave the empire; and Baghdad, conquered in 1534 by Sulaymān, was occupied by the Safavids only temporarily, from 1623 to 1638, the date of the Murād campaign.

The larger Arab cities show, moreover, in their very structure, a trace of this long-lasting inclusion in an empire that was vast, powerful, and relatively well protected from outside aggression. With the exception of Baghdad and Mosul, which had to be protected against renewed attacks from the Persians (like the attempts of Nādir Šāh against Baghdad in 1733 and Mosul in 1743), and of Algiers, always in danger from seaborne perils, Arab cities had no need of those important fortifications that would have been required by a threat from the outside. Though ancient cities preserved, and sometimes restored, the old town walls, vast unprotected suburbs developed around Cairo (to the south and to the west of the Fatimid town), Damascus (the Mīdān suburb), and Aleppo (the northern and eastern suburbs); Tunis built an important exterior fortified wall much later, toward the end of the eighteenth century, in response to an "interior" threat, the aggressiveness of Tunisia's Algerian neighbors.

The Ottomans set up a fairly homogeneous governmental system over this huge political network. Around 1609 the Arab domains made up 12 *wilāya* (provinces) out of a total of 36: Yemen, Basra, Baghdad, Mosul, Raqqa, Aleppo, Damascus, eastern Tripoli, Misr (Egypt), western Tripoli, Tunis, Algiers; their capitals are the cities that we shall study.[1] Local government rested essentially on three elements: a governor *(wālī)* with the rank of pasha, militias, the main one being the Janissaries; and a judicial organization under the control of a *qāḍī* (judge) appointed by Istanbul. But, in many places, the Ottoman organization left a large role to local elites; a most illustrative example of this integration is given by the Egyptian Mamluks who, in Cairo, formed the fourth base of power.

1.2. The Provinces

The administrative control of Istanbul over such vast, varied, and heterogeneous territories did, however, adapt to local autonomies. Probably little desirous of governing this gigantic entity directly—and undoubtedly unable to do so—the central government often limited itself to controlling the interplay of local powers from a distance. It attempted, from time to time, to regain a firmer hold on some of the provinces by military intervention (as in the cases of Tunis in 1708 and Egypt in 1786) or by the appointment of "nonlocal" pashas (as at Mosul in 1756 and 1760). But, generally speaking, the Sublime Porte often resigned itself to leaving real local authority to groups or individuals, so long as order was fairly well maintained and the tribute was levied regularly.

The sultans thus accepted developments that resulted in the installation of more or less autonomous regional governments. Their juxtaposition formed, in the eighteenth century, a very varied picture where there could be seen every shade of subordination right up to the Sublime Porte, from direct administration to near independence, so much so that the Ottoman Empire must be regarded as a "commonwealth" rather than as a highly centralized political entity. In any case, one can truly appreciate the relationship between the Sublime Porte and local authorities only by taking into account the subtle game that was played between them. On the one hand, the central government resigned itself to provincial autonomies insofar as the essentials (Ottoman suzerainty) were preserved and the major objectives of Ottoman policy (e.g., exterior security) were attained; on the other hand, local authorities respected exterior patterns and certain realities so as to ensure the real enjoyment of the political and material fruits of autonomy.[2]

It would obviously be impractical to attempt to enumerate in detail the forms taken by these autonomies, for doing so would mean presenting the history of all the provinces of the empire.[3] Let us simply say that the province of Aleppo was undoubtedly the only one governed, more or less constantly, by pashas sent by the Porte. Even so, these pashas had to put up with the conflicts that, in the struggle for power, locally opposed two strong pressure groups, the sharifs and the Janissaries, both deeply rooted in the local population.

In some regions, local authorities developed while leaving an appearance of subordination relatively intact. "Mamluk" emirs formed a kind of dynasty in Baghdad, from Hasan Pasha (1704–1723) on, and they succeeded each other, nearly without a break, until 1831. In Algiers, after a period of struggle for government control between the ship captains *(raʾīs)* and the Janissaries, the latter finally gained the upper hand. The Janissaries established, from 1659 on, a sort of collective power, which maintained, however, an appearance of submission to the Porte. In the eighteenth century the "deys" of Algiers evolved toward a nearly monarchical form of government of, in some instances, near hereditary nature. In Egypt the pashas' authority was rapidly eclipsed by the Mamluks and the Janissaries. The latter dominated from 1660 to 1760; then houses *(bayt)* of beys managed to impose their authority, and at certain times governmental power evolved in the direction of a monarchy (ᶜAlī Bey, 1760–1772; Muḥammad Bey, 1772–1775; Ismāᶜīl Bey, 1786–1791) or a duumvirate (Murād and Ibrāhīm Bey, 1791–1798). The very appearance of subordination to the Sublime Porte was not always respected. ᶜAlī Bey asserted himself as an independent ruler, and during the last decades of the eighteenth century the tribute *(ḫazīna)* was paid very irregularly; indeed, sometimes not at all.

Near dynasties were established in Damascus, with the ᶜAẓm family that took over power (with some interruptions) between 1725 and 1783, maintaining a veritable reign during the time of Asᶜad Pasha (1743–1757); and in Mosul, where another "local" family, that of the Ǧalīlī, established its authority as early as 1726, when Ismāᶜīl al-Ǧalīlī became pasha of the province. The Ǧalīlī stayed in power nearly continuously until 1834, in spite of several attempts by the Porte to import foreign pashas to Mosul.

Last, in North Africa, actual dynasties were installed that retained only exterior signs of subordination to the Porte, whose authority was reduced to granting, rather automatically, the title of pasha to the rulers brought to power by heredity; thus, Tunisia had two successive dynasties of "beys," first from the Muradite family, in the seventeenth century, and then from the Husaynite family, during the eighteenth and nineteenth centuries. From 1711 on, Tripoli was governed by the Qaramanlī family, whose authority did not end until well into the nineteenth century, when the Ottoman Porte succeeded in reinstalling its authority in Tripoli (1835) at about the same time that it did in Baghdad and Mosul.

The comparative flexibility with which the Ottoman government accepted very different local situations is, in the last analysis, one of the factors that explains the amazingly long life of an empire that was born in 1516, as far as the Arab world was concerned, and did not really start to collapse until 1830, with the conquest of Algeria by France.

2. URBAN EXPANSION DURING THE OTTOMAN PERIOD

2.1. Urban Expansion

The Ottoman period is usually considered an era of general decline, in particular with regard to urban life. By stressing the partitioning of urban life, with the *millet* system,[4] Ottoman domination is said to have resulted in a veritable dislocation of the urban structure; indeed, in an anarchy that brought about the irremediable decadence of the city. Two quotations will suffice to characterize this conception:

• M. Clerget: Under the Ottomans, Cairo "is dying slowly and imperceptibly; it withdraws into itself, letting the ruins of its glorious past slowly crumble down. . . . Cairo goes back . . . to the dispersed population that the first Arabs were attached to . . . the growing disorder of the urban layout, difficult communications also mirror the political and economic anarchy."

• J. Sauvaget: In Aleppo, under the Ottomans, "the elements of disintegration . . . are apparent here again, with a tendency to exaggeration that accelerates the dissociation of the urban center into separate compartments. . . . Ottoman Aleppo is nothing but a 'trompe-l'oeil,' a sumptuous facade behind which there is nothing left but ruins."[5]

These catastrophic points of view are so obviously in contradiction with an easily observable reality, and they are belied in so evident a manner by J. Sauvaget's own research on Aleppo, that one can only be surprised that the development of the main Arab cities between the sixteenth and the nineteenth centuries has been ignored for so long.[6]

This urban progress is apparent in the extension of built-up areas that, in many cities, took the form of vast suburbs developing along the main commercial routes, outside the *intra-muros* town. The surface area of Mamluk Cairo, at the time of its apogee, probably did not exceed 450 hectares; the built-up area of Cairo, according to the *Description de l'Egypte,* totaled 662 hectares;[7] Damascus, grew from 212 hectares at the beginning of the sixteenth century to 313 hectares around the middle of the nineteenth century; Aleppo, from 238 hectares toward 1516 to 367 hectares at the beginning of the

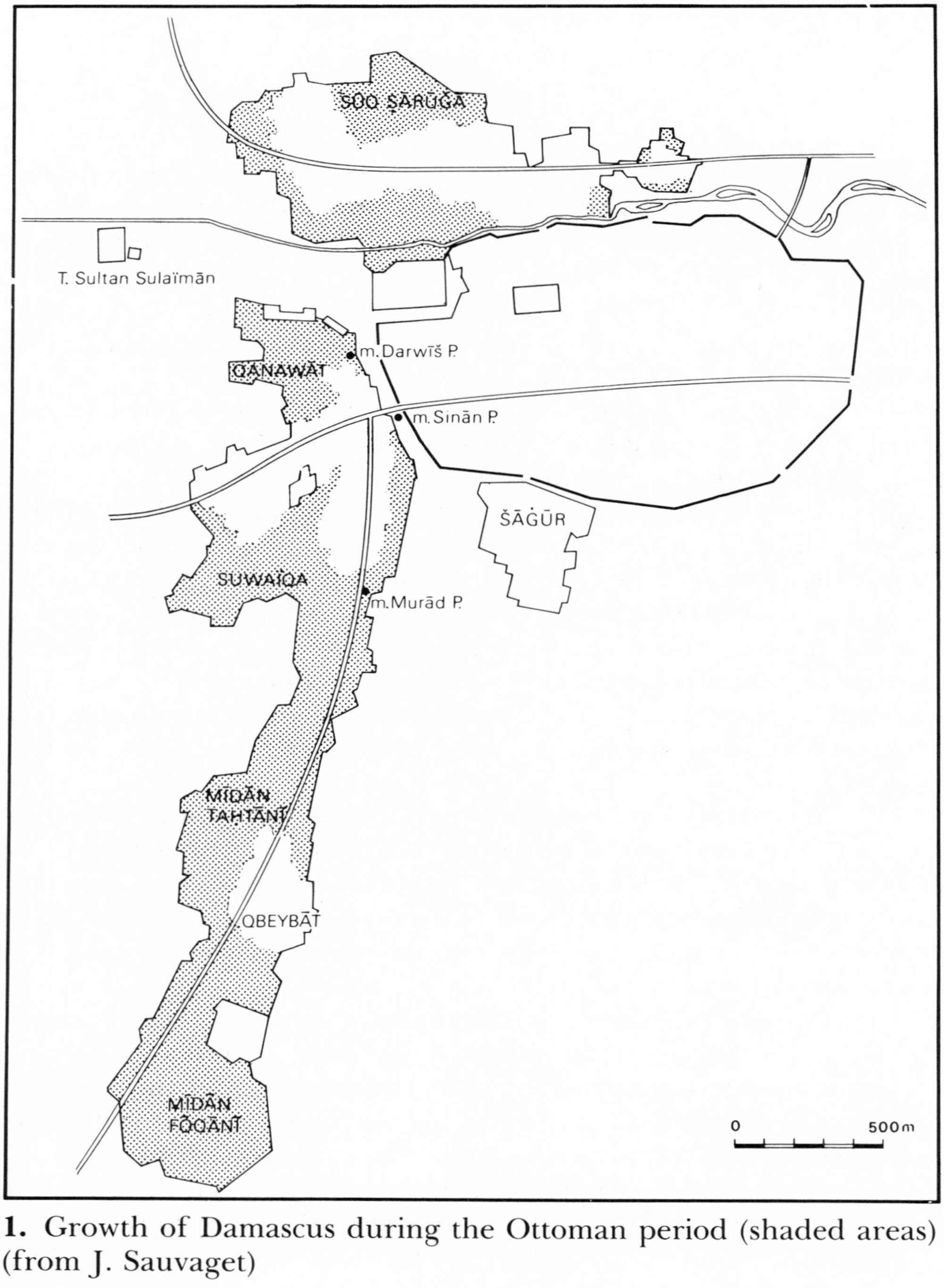
SŪQ ṢĀRŪǦĀ
T. Sultan Sulaïmān
m. Darwīš P.
QANAWĀT
m. Sinān P.
ŠĀĠŪR
SUWAÏQA
m. Murād P.
MĪDĀN
TAḤTĀNĪ
QBEYBĀT
MĪDĀN
FŌQĀNĪ
0
500m

1. Growth of Damascus during the Ottoman period (shaded areas) (from J. Sauvaget)

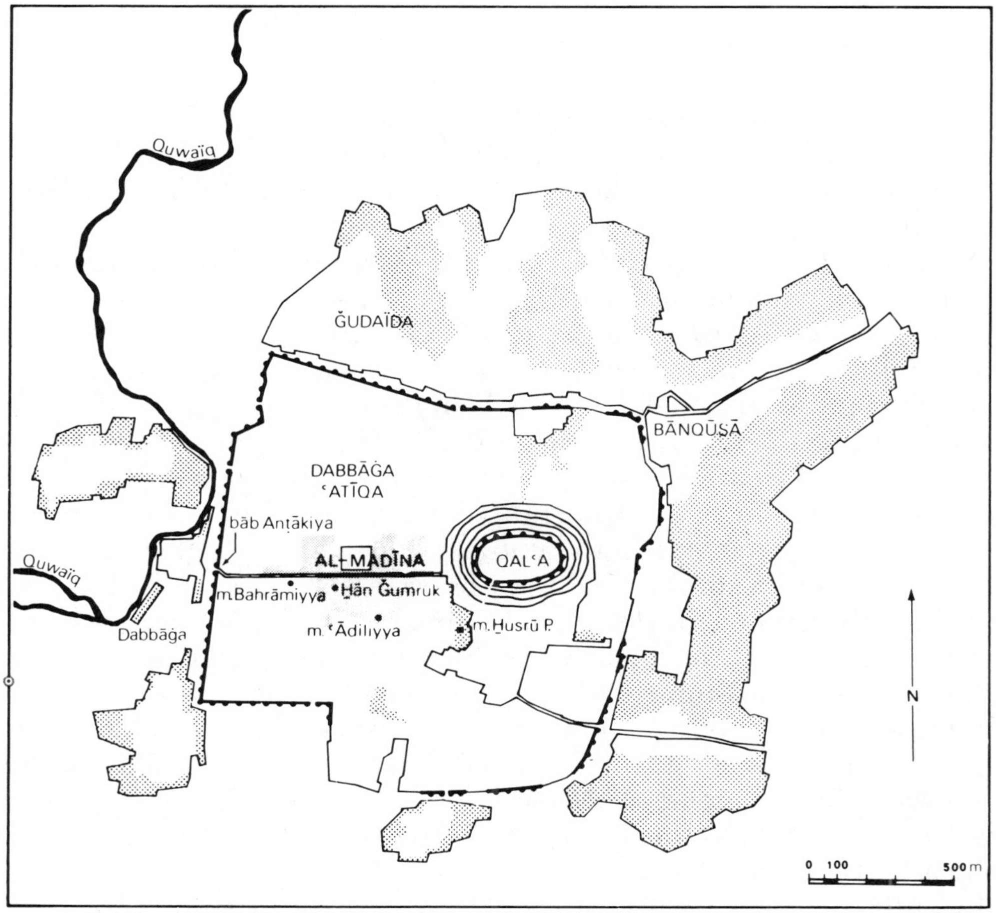
Quwaïq
ĞUDAÏDA
BĀNQŪSĀ
DABBĀĠA
ʿATĪQA
bāb Anṭākiya
Quwaïq
AL-MADĪNA
QALʿA
m.Bahrāmiyya
•Ḫān Ğumruk
m. ʿĀdiliyya
m.Ḫusrū P.
Dabbāġa
N
0 100 500 m

2. Growth of Aleppo during the Ottoman period (shaded areas) (from J. Sauvaget)

nineteenth century.[8] In the three cases, growth was around 50%. Recently proposed estimates of the populations of these towns follow the same ascendant curve. For Cairo, I have suggested an estimated 150,000 inhabitants in 1517; 263,000 inhabitants is the figure given by the scholars of the *Description* toward 1800. A. Abdel Nour reckons that in Damascus the population increased from 52,000 at the end of the sixteenth century to 90,000 at the end of the eighteenth century; and, in Aleppo, from 60,000 toward 1570 to 120,000 toward 1790.[9] These impressions are confirmed by what we know of the towns' commercial structures, particularly caravanserais.

How can one explain an urban development that is just as impressive in other towns such as Algiers, a truly Ottoman creation, or Tunis, where expansion was especially pronounced during the eighteenth century?[10]

Let us first note that the Ottoman conquest had been preceded by a period of general decline, which inevitably had to be followed by an era of restoration at a time when exhausted states (those of the Hafsids, Mamluks, etc.) were succeeded by a powerful empire. Towns that historians describe as being ruined during the fifteenth and sixteenth centuries (such as Baghdad after the Mongol conquest, Damascus after Tamerlane, Cairo after the crises of 1348 and of the beginning of the fifteenth century, Tunis after the Spanish occupations of the sixteenth century) knew a respite that, even by itself, would explain the recovery observed.

On the other hand, the establishment of an immense Mediterranean empire (2.5 million square kilometers, the largest political unit since the Roman Empire) created an enormous market where both individuals and products could circulate freely from the frontiers of Morocco to those of Iran, from the steppes of southern Russia to Abyssinia. The centers located on the main commercial routes (which was the case of most of the big Arab cities) could only benefit from the activity of these interior currents, which would remain dominant up until the eighteenth century. The vitality of Oriental trade was not really interrupted by the entry of Europeans into the Indian Ocean, and the appearance of a new product such as coffee afterward gave it an enormous expansion.

A symbol of the strength of these interior currents, the pilgrimage *(ḥaǧǧ)* took on a heretofore unprecedented importance during the Ottoman era. The very dimensions of the empire, its political unification, and the efforts engaged in by the Ottoman government and its local representatives to facilitate the fulfillment of the *ḥaǧǧ* made possible the travel of caravans of pilgrims difficult to number but estimated at 30,000 or 40,000 for those converging on Cairo and at 20,000 to 30,000 for those assembling in Damascus. To the exchange of goods directly induced by the moving of these human masses alone during a trip that lasted one year was added the commercial activity carried out through the medium of the caravans, on the way to the Hedjaz and back, which concerned the most distant regions of the empire.[11]

The creation of the empire and the comparative tolerance of the Ottoman authorities finally resulted in an increasing importance of national and religious groups, the number and variety of which contributed to the development of urban activity. It is enough to mention here the role played by the Jewish and Christian communities more or less everywhere; the installation of Turkish communities, both powerful and big consumers of luxury goods in the various capitals, along with the new authorities; and the tens of thousands of Andalusian émigrants who were accepted in North African towns, particularly from 1609 on, and who greatly contributed to the cities' economic expansion. In a metropolis such as Cairo, at the end of the eighteenth century, there were—apart from 10,000 Copts and 10,000 members of the dominant caste—25,000 "foreign" Muslims (Turks, Syrians, and Maghribians) and 15,000 minority peoples (Jews, Greeks, Syrians, Armenians), that is, more than 60,000 persons out of a total population of 263,000.[12] During the sixteenth and seventeenth centuries, Algiers and Tunis had several thousand Turks (Janissaries in particular); converts (the so-called renegades); and Andalusians, Jews, and members of outside communities (called *barrānī* in Algiers) of an extreme variety.[13] Arab cities were, during the Ottoman era, more cosmopolitan than they had ever been before. Ottoman relative liberalism on this point, and the comparative efficiency of the self-governing system of the *millet* certainly contributed to a large extent to the cities' economic development, as is demonstrated by the well-known examples of *šawwāšiyya* (capmakers) craftmanship, invigorated by the Andalusians in Tunis and by the spectacular expansion of the Christian community in the Ǧudayda quarter of Aleppo [A. F 12].

3. CHARACTERISTICS OF ARAB CITIES IN THE OTTOMAN ERA

Considering the fairly homogeneous geographical area we are concerned with (the Arab region of the empire, from Algeria to Iraq) and the relatively limited period involved (sixteenth to eighteenth centuries), and considering also the obvious community of cultural, socioeconomic, and historical factors, we may expect the cities that are under study (mainly Algiers, Tunis, Cairo, Damascus, Aleppo, Mosul, and Baghdad)[14] to reveal enough common features so that general characteristics can be defined.

3.1. Public City and Private City

The phenomenon that seems fundamental is the pronounced differentiation apparent in all these great cities between districts of large-scale economic activity (dominated by big international trade) and residential districts. This differentiation appears to be a sociocultural feature, based in part on religious conceptions—but in part only—for the relative segregation of family life is also a Mediterranean phenomenon that extends beyond the Islamic domain. This conception of a distinctly divided space, of a *public* city as opposed to a *private* city, can be read on town plans where two types of street network appear quite clearly. In the central zone of the town, given over to economic activities, relatively wide, regular, open streets form a network extending without a break to the town limits. This network is a legacy of antiquity in those cases where an Arab city succeeded a Roman one (Aleppo, Damascus); but it can also be noted in cities that were founded by the Arabs. (e.g., Cairo). In the private, or residential, districts, one finds an irregular network of a type that is generally considered to be a characteristic of the "Arab" town but that actually forms only a part of the street system of the city.[15] This division of urban space was, moreover, clearly perceived, and described, by Muslim jurists, as Baber Johansen's recent work perfectly shows.[16] This differentiation, in spite of the great complexity of the plan in its detail, makes the structure of the town fully legible on the overall maps.

3.2. The Centers

Two consequences arise from this fundamental character of the Arab city. The first concerns the high concentration of economic activity in the town center. Whatever the dimensions of the town, and even in the case of a metropolis like Cairo (250,000 inhabitants in the eighteenth century), or of such cities as Aleppo, Damascus, or

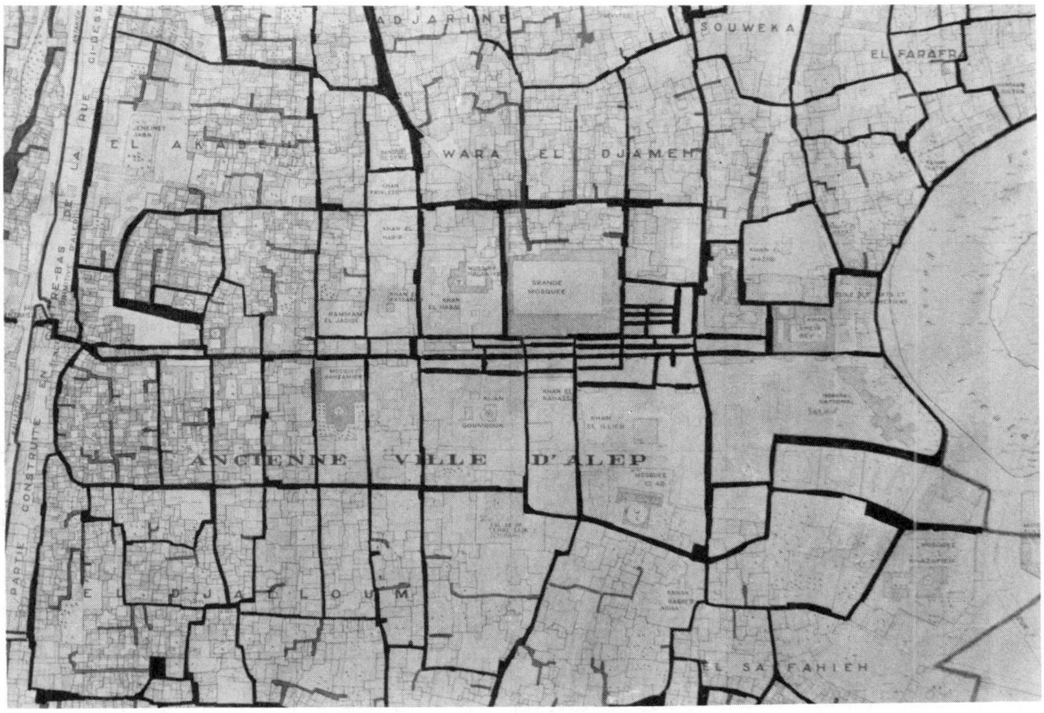
ADJARINE
SOUWEKA
EL FARAFRA
EL AKABEH
WARA EL DJAMEH
GRANDE MOSQUEE
ANCIENNE VILLE D'ALEP
EL DJALLOUM
EL SAFAHIEH
PARTIE CONSTRUITE EN CONTRE-BAS DE LA RUE CI-DESSUS

3. Aleppo city center (Madīna)

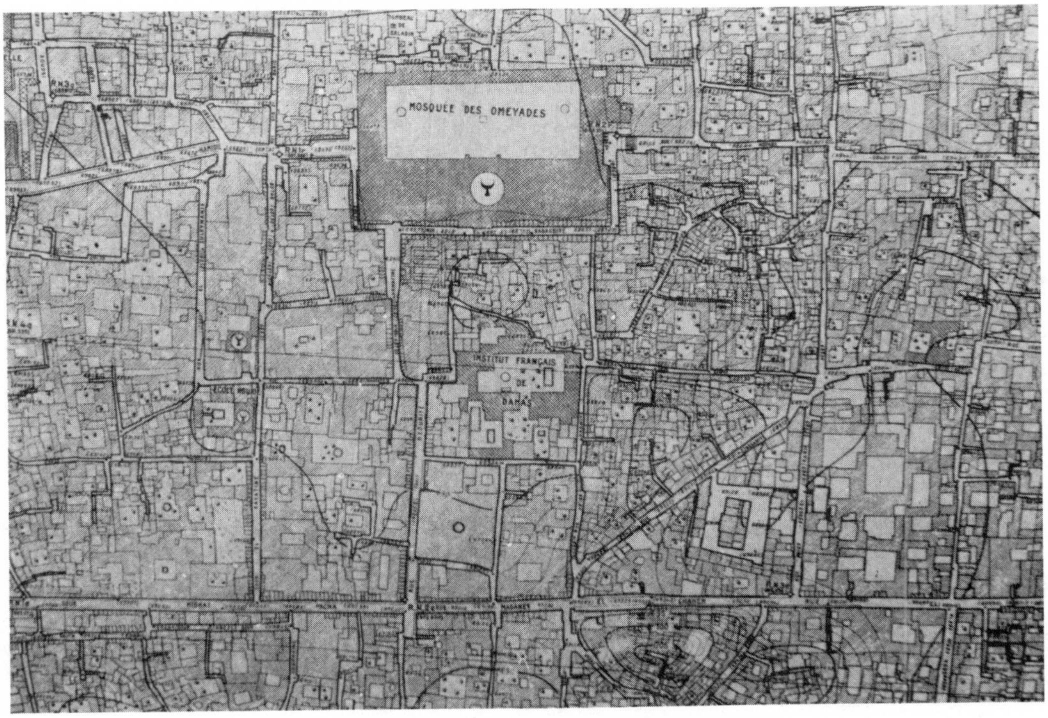
MOSQUÉE DES OMEYADES
INSTITUT FRANÇAIS DE DAMAS

4. Damascus city center

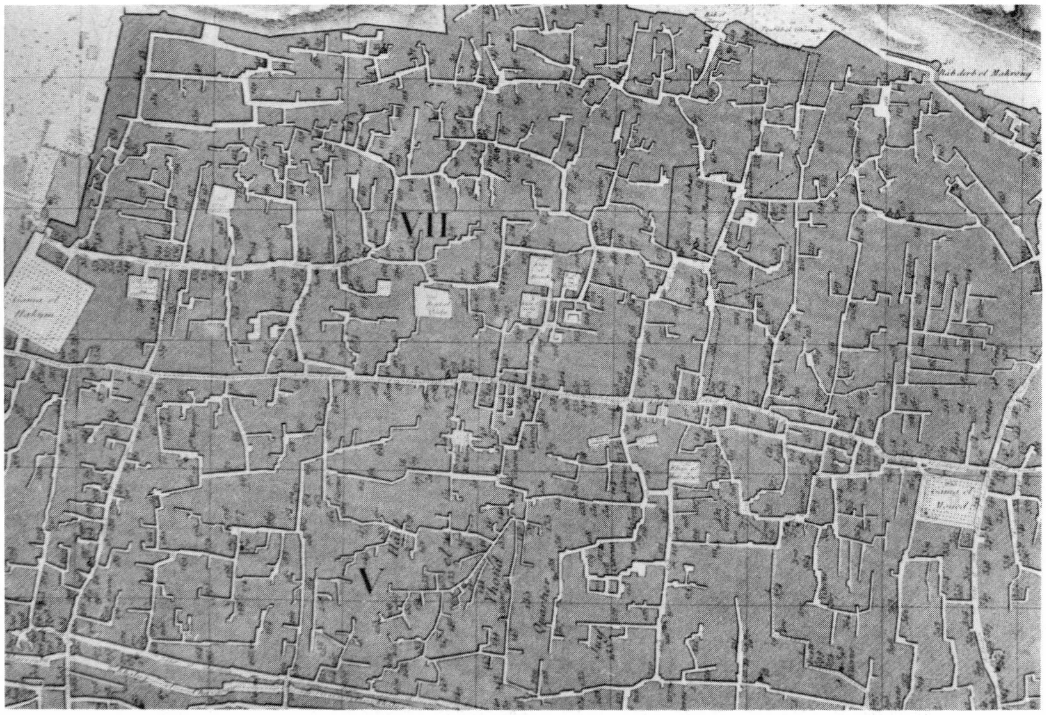
VII
V

5. Cairo city center (Qāhira) (From the *Description de l'Egypte*)

Baghdad (between 100,000 and 150,000), main economic activities—chiefly the big international trade that took place in the principal caravanserais (called khan, *wakāla*, or *funduq*, according to the region)—were grouped in a relatively limited zone. This concentration, already very conspicuous in medieval times, persisted during the Ottoman era with the development of the *bedestan* (center for international trade) in the core of the city.

Louis Massignon has shown the close relationship that existed between the central region of markets and the Great Mosque, and in particular the frequent location of the *ṣāġa* (goldsmiths' market and exchange center) and the *sūq al-ġazl* (thread market) in the immediate vicinity of the main mosque.[17] The relative fixedness of the markets (suqs), also noted by L. Massignon, is a consequence of the relative lack of evolution of techniques and economic life from the end of the medieval period till modern times. But it is important to note that, with regard to particulars, many changes in market localization eventually took place over the centuries. These changes are highly significant, as they mark the decline of old commercial activities and the appearance of new ones. As such, they should be studied with care, for they are often unique evidences of the evolution of economic activities.

Thus, in the structuring of urban centers, the market and the Great Mosque played the decisive role, that of the political center being generally limited, if not nonexistent. In all great cities there is a complete identification between the suq quarter and the "city center." The concentration of the markets is so intense that E. Wirth suggests that the suq is "the only . . . distinctive criterion for the Near Eastern city which can be considered as an Islamic cultural heritage."[18]

3.3. Radioconcentric Character of the City

The second aspect of this intense urban centralization is that the town's activities developed by radiating outward from the zone of the markets and the Great Mosque. Roughly, the localization of activities, from the center, had a radioconcentric character, the economic activities being arranged in successive rings according to their importance, but also, in a negative way, according to the inconvenience they brought about, or to their need of space. Nearest to the center were to be found the main activities, generally the most specialized (e.g., international trade in spices and coffee, in expensive cloth); the poorer and less differentiated activities—those requiring close contact with the rural world, those demanding vast open spaces, and those causing the greatest nuisance to neighboring inhabitants—tended to be pushed toward the outskirts of the town. The list of these outlying activities is fairly constant from one town to another: vegetable, fruit, and grain markets; livestock markets, slaughterhouses, tanneries, kilns and the like. The residential zones generally followed the same type of concentric layout, radiating from the central market zone.

However, this concentric disposition in successive rings (which roughly matches the diagram suggested by E. W. Burgess,[19] but with a quite different layout in the location of the residential zones) was rarely achieved in a perfect or complete manner. Geographical, historical, or economic factors often disrupted the steady development of this spatial organization. In particular, one can mention the following:

• The uneven development of the town in various directions, as in Cairo, Damascus, Aleppo, Algiers, and Tunis. It brought about a more or less pronounced decentering of the economic "center" that, in all these cases, no longer occupies the topographical center of the city. In the case of a "round" town like Mosul, the economic center took the shape of a "circular sector" that widens from its summit (near the Great Mosque) in the direction of the bridge on the Tigris. Such division into sectors recalls H. Hoyt's diagram;[20] it is carried out, less distinctly than in the case of Mosul, in several Arab towns (e.g., in Algiers).

• The development of secondary activity centers, in the most important towns. It led to more complex, polynuclear structures (in this case, see the multinuclei scheme of C. D. Harris and E. L. Ullman)[21] that are to be found in Cairo and Aleppo. The removal of the political and military center outside the economic center was often at the origin of the creation of those secondary nuclei with "under-the-Citadel" *(taḥt al-Qalʿa)* quarters that exist in Cairo, Damascus, and Aleppo.

• The utilization of peripheral space, in areas where land is more easily available than in the overpopulated center, for the development of wealthy residential districts, located between zones that were generally devoted either to the artisanal or commercial activities mentioned above or to the housing of the poorer part of the population.

3.4. The Residential Quarters

The development of more or less closed residential quarters, along with the existence of a highly differentiated business center, appears to be the other fundamental characteristic of the Arab town in the modern period. Under various names (*ḥawma* in the Maghrib; *ḥāra* in Cairo and Damascus; *maḥalla* in Aleppo, Mosul, and Baghdad), these quarters have a somewhat similar appearance and structure from Morocco to Iraq. Connected with the principal network of town streets by a main way *(darb)*, which often gave its name to the quarter itself (hence the very numerous names beginning

"Darb-al" for the quarters of Cairo), and served by a hierarchical organization of smaller streets usually ending in culs-de-sac, these quarters formed unities that were often completely closed. They were placed under the authority of shaykhs who, given the limited dimensions of the quarters (generally a maximum of 4 or 5 hectares, often much less, with a population of 1,000 to 2,000 inhabitants, that is, 200 to 400 families), were able to exercise effective and efficient control over the entire population in the *ḥāra*.

In this zone of residential quarters a complex and irregular network of streets and dead ends developed.[22] Traffic flow (which was mainly pedestrian) was oriented to, and from, the center where the specialized markets stood, as well as the main places of worship, which were also the gathering centers of the population. The inhabitants of the quarters went to the center where they worked in their shops, or where they provided for needs that could not be supplied by local markets *(suwayqa)*. They returned to their homes by using the same street network. These quarters made up "pockets," so to speak, that opened only toward the interior of the town: connections between the economic and religious center with the exterior of the town were provided by a few main radial roads, up to the town gates, and farther to the suburbs that eventually developed along these main axes, as can clearly be seen on a plan of Cairo or Aleppo.

The statistical importance of the dead ends (nearly 50% of the total street network length in towns such as Algiers, Cairo, Damascus, and Aleppo) is quite remarkable, and it is obviously a characteristic feature of these Mediterranean cities. The problem of the origins of this system, which totally distinguishes Arab towns from Greco-Roman and Occidental medieval cities, has not yet been solved. E. Wirth's suggestion of an Oriental origin remains to be confirmed; in ancient Oriental towns archaeological research has been turned, nearly exclusively, to the study of urban centers, a situation that hardly allows any definite conclusion concerning their general planning as our knowledge stands at present. However, there is no question that the system of closed quarters and dead ends, besides the ingenious solution it provided for the problem of security, enabled such perfect fulfillment of the ideals of a society dominated by Islam, in ensuring nearly total isolation of family life, that one is of course tempted to see it as a "Muslim" characteristic of the city. Yet, under these conditions, how can one explain the apparent exception of Iraqi towns where the *maḥalla* are generally open, in a region (Mesopotamia) where the influence of antiquity deeply marked the character of urban evolution, and where the influence of Islam followed the same lines as in Mediterranean Arab countries? Better knowledge of the actual conditions under which the quarters structure developed, at the time of the foundation of the towns (e.g., to allow for the installation of military contingents in Cairo); a more comprehensive comparison with similar systems existing elsewhere in the Islamic domain (Ottoman towns, Irano-Afghan towns), and more precise information about the structure of pre-Islamic "classical" and Arab towns would undoubtedly help to remove some of these uncertainties.[23]

In conclusion, it is probable that this organization into quarters, which permitted strict control of the subjects while leaving them with a certain amount of autonomy, was strengthened with the advent of the Ottomans. It corresponded perfectly to their "decentralized" conception of administration and government. The structure of the historical sectors of the Arab towns we know about was deeply marked by the development of the quarters, whose number undoubtedly greatly increased in Ottoman times, accompanying the urban expansion that characterized at least a part of that period. The example of Cairo, with its double frontier of *ḥāra* on the western limits of the town, is absolutely demonstrative of this point of view: the most easterly line, near the Canal (Ḫalīǧ), would correspond to the extreme extension of the town in this direction at the end of the Mamluk period; the westernmost line of *ḥāra,* on the limits of the Ottoman town, would correspond to the ultimate development of Cairo in this direction during this period (see Ill. 27).

3.5. The Judicial Institution and the Waqf

One must also retain as one of the essential characteristics of Arab towns in modern times the important role played by two specifically Islamic institutions, the justice rendered by the *qāḍī* and the *waqf.*

3.5.1 The judges *(qāḍī)* engaged in activities in such varied areas of Muslim society that one can say, without exaggeration, that no aspect of the religious, social, or economic life of the population was outside their jurisdiction. In the towns, the courts of the judges were, in the last instance, the authority before which all the problems of urban people were normally settled: relations of the inhabitants among themselves and with the authorities, professional activities, questions concerning urban administration. Robert Brunschvig, in a classic article, showed that the medieval judges of the Maghrib of the Malikite school had worked out, at least in an implicit manner, principles in urban matters.[24] The research recently carried out by Baber Johansen,[25] mainly on more modern Hanafite legal texts, shows that these principles continued to develop. It is in the countless court *(maḥākim)* registers *(daftar)* that one finds its daily application during the Ottoman era. Very little study has been carried out in this field, but the few soundings made in research work like that of Galal El-Nahal clearly show the variety of the judges' activity, and the importance of their intervention in strictly urban matters, ranging from building regulations (e.g., on such concerns as security, nuisances, or protection of privacy), to problems connected with the organization of the quarters *(ḥāra),* to management of the guilds, and so on.[26] It is also likely that during the Ottoman period the traditional functions of the judges in this domain were strengthened, enabling them to play a decisive role in problems concerning the town.

3.5.2 Just as remarkable in the organization of urban space is the importance of another typically Muslim institution, the *waqf* ("habous" in the Maghrib). The basic principles of the *waqf* are well known: a pious intention expressed in an endowment for religious or charitable purposes, or for social work; the perpetuity and inalienability of funds incorporated into the *waqf,* only the income being assigned to the pious deeds (the final beneficiaries of the foundation); the existence of two kinds of *waqf,* the charitable *waqf (ḫayrī),* the total income of which immediately goes to pious, charitable, or public utility work, and the family *waqf (ahlī)* whose income, intended in the last instance for charity, is first distributed, in part, to the donor *(wāqif),* and, after him, to the successors he has designated in the deed *(waqfiyya).* For various reasons, the *waqf* was widely used during the Ottoman era. It is estimated that in Egypt, in 1920, 18,500 urban buildings were held by *waqf;* in the town of Algiers, in 1830, half of the buildings were habous.[27]

In order to reach their objectives, both public (the maintenance of religious or charitable buildings or of public utility foundations) and private (the protection of private property or incomes provided for by the foundation), the great *waqf* often took the form of large-scale endeavors, grouping generally around the pious foundation to be maintained, a number of buildings of commercial character (shops, caravanserais, public baths). The incomes of these buildings were designed to bring about the realization of the aims fixed by the *waqf*. Therefore, the constitution of large urban *waqf* often gave rise, in periods of urban expansion, to urban operations for which the *waqf* provided the legal framework and the necessary financing. It was in the context of the *waqf* that urban development took place in the Madīna ("City") of Aleppo in the sixteenth century, and in the southern part of Cairo around the middle of the seventeenth century.[28]

Through the activity of the *qāḍī* and the system of the *waqf*, Muslim legislation therefore provided efficient means for ensuring the administration of the city and for organizing its expansion. In both cases, the Ottoman era coincided with the development of the role played by these institutions.

3.6. Community Organizations

Last, Arab cities in the Ottoman era were characterized by the existence of a great diversity of community organizations *(ṭāʾifa,* pl. *ṭawāʾif)* that played a very important role in the most varied domains: professional communities (craftsmen's and traders' guilds), religious and national communities (minority groups—Christians, Jews, and "foreign" Muslims), and geographical communities (in the quarters already mentioned). Each of these communities was placed under the authority of a shaykh and came to play a considerable social and administrative role in city life. These *ṭawāʾif* provided a framework that ensured the inner cohesion of urban society while enabling the authorities to exercise firm control (in an indirect way) over the subjects *(raʿiya).* The subjects were thus integrated in a series of networks that covered every aspect of their lives and that, in most cases, were superimposed: a given individual belonged to a craft guild in the course of his professional activity in the suq where he worked during the day, and he belonged to the community of the quarter in which he lived with his family. These basic cells of economic and social life in the cities were quite numerous; they were, therefore, of limited size, a fact that ensured very close social and administrative control over the population. In Cairo there were approximately 250 craft guilds for an active population of about 100,000 craftsmen and tradesmen (of total city population of 250,000) and nearly 100 *ḥāra,* where between 100,000 and 150,000 people lived. In Aleppo at the end of the seventeenth century there were around 130 guilds and 75 *maḥalla* (for a total population of about 100,000). These basic components of the city were strictly compartmentalized and did not fit into any hierarchy; generally, there was no central organization to provide control over the craft guilds, except perhaps in Tunis and Mosul. A "shaykh al-mashaykh" (shaykh of the shaykhs) did not exist in Damascus before the nineteenth century; the quarters were not organized at the city level, and they constituted totally autonomous structures, except again in Tunis where three shaykhs were in charge of the administration of the Madīna (walled city) and of the two suburbs of Bāb Ǧazīra and Bāb Suwayqa, which involved control of the quarter shaykhs (called here *muḥarrik).* As a result, this urban society, though highly structured, was unable to produce "popular" counterpowers that could have challenged the central political authorities and thus enable the city to evolve toward the creation of "communes," as existed in the West.

These various institutions did exist in the Arab towns before the Ottoman era, but it seems that a result of Ottoman rule was their strengthening so that they could provide the means of controlling the very numerous and diverse populations of the empire. Given the sheer extent of the Ottoman dominions and the great ethnic and religious variety of their provinces, the Ottomans, rather than try to set up a centralized administration that they would probably have been incapable of devising and operating, preferred to leave a fair amount of autonomy to national, religious, and professional groups and to use the *ṭawāʾif* as an intermediary for anything that concerned administration (especially financial) of the *raʿiya.* What today one would call "public services" (e.g., water supply, urban transport, street cleaning) were provided, in Cairo, at least, by guilds of specialized trades (with the contribution of the *waqf* in some cases: the *sabīl,* or public fountains, were generally maintained by *waqf*).

This system, a very original one if we compare it with those we know in Europe, helped to solve, for three centuries, the contradiction that existed between the apparent underadministration of the towns and the necessity of fulfilling the fundamental needs of their inhabitants; and it allowed for the organization of the urban expansion that took place during that period.

Notes

1. Donald Edgar Pitcher, *An Historical Geography of the Ottoman Empire* (Leiden, 1972).

2. See the significative cases of Mosul (Percy Kemp, "Mosul and Mosuli Historians of the Jalīlī Era. 1726–1834," thesis, Oxford University, 1979); of Damascus (Abdul-Karim Rafeq, *The Province of Damascus, 1723–1783* [Beirut, 1966]; Karl K. Barbir, *Ottoman Rule in Damascus. 1708–1758* [Princeton, 1980]); and of Tunis (Mohamed H. Cherif, "Pouvoir et société dans la Tunisie de H'usayn Bin ʿAli. 1705–1740," thesis, University of Paris, 1979).

3. See P. M. Holt, *Egypt and the Fertile Crescent. 1516–1922* (Ithaca, N.Y., 1966); Herbert L. Bodman, *Political Factions in Aleppo (1760–1826)* (Chapel Hill, N.C., 1963); Stephen H. Longrigg, *Four Centuries of Modern Iraq* (Oxford, 1925); H. de Grammont, *Histoire d'Alger sous la domination turque* (Angers, France, 1887); and the studies mentioned in note 2.

4. On the *millet* (organization of the religious minorities in semiautonomous communities) see B. Braude and B. Lewis, eds., *Christians and Jews in the Ottoman Empire,* 2 vols. (New York, 1982).

5. Marcel Clerget, *Le Caire,* 2 vols. (Cairo, 1934), I, 178; Jean Sauvaget, *Alep. Essai sur le développement d'une grande ville syrienne, des origines au milieu du XIXe siècle,* 2 vols. (Paris, 1941), I, 238–239.

6. About these stereotypes and their necessary revision see André Raymond, "La conquête ottomane et le développement des grandes villes arabes," *Revue de l'Occident Musulman et de la Méditerranée* 27, no. 1 (1979); and K. Barbir, *Damascus,* p. 5.

7. André Raymond, "Le Caire sous les Ottomans," in Bernard Maury, André Raymond, Jacques Revault, and Mona Zakariya, *Palais et maisons du Caire, II, Epoque ottomane* (Paris, 1983).

8. Figures taken from Jean Sauvaget's plans in "Esquisse d'une histoire de la ville de Damas," *Revue des Etudes Islamiques (REI)* (1954), plans VIII and X; and *Alep,* Album plans LXII and LXX.

9. Antoine Abdel Nour, *Introduction à l'histoire urbaine de la Syrie ottomane (XVIe–XVIIIe siècle)* (Beirut, 1982), 73–74 and 66–70.

10. Where this urban expansion led to a transfer of the tanneries in the eigh-

teenth century, a phenomenon that also took place in Aleppo (sixteenth century) and in Cairo (end of the sixteenth century). See André Raymond, "Le déplacement des tanneries à Alep, au Caire et à Tunis, à l'époque ottomane," *Revue d'Histoire Maghrébine* (1977), 7–8.

11. On the *ḥağğ* see A. Rafeq, *Province,* 8, 52, 73, 97; K. Barbir, *Damascus,* 125, 134, 155; A. Raymond, "Conquête ottomane," 119–120.

12. André Raymond, *Artisans et commerçants au Caire au XVIIIème siècle,* 2 vols. (Damascus, 1974), II 451–501.

13. For Algiers see Pierre Boyer, *La vie quotidienne à Alger à la veille de l'intervention française* (Paris, 1963), 127–149.

14. See the bibliography for some of the studies on these cities.

15. On the double street system see André Raymond, "Remarques sur la voirie des grandes villes arabes," in *Proceedings of the 10th Congress of the UEAI* (Edinburgh, 1982).

16. Baber Johansen, "Eigentum, Familie und Obrigkeit im hanafitischen Strafrecht," *Die Welt des Islams* 19 (1979); "The Claims of Men and the Claims of God," *Pluriformiteit en verdeling van de macht in het Midden-Oosten* 4 (1980); and "The All-Embracing Town and Its Mosques," *Revue de l'Occident Musulman et de la Méditerranée* 32, no. 2 (1981).

17. Louis Massignon, *Mission en Mésopotamie (1907–1908),* 2 vols. (Cairo, 1912), II 90–92.

18. On the role of the suq as a decisive element in the organization of the Arab city see Eugen Wirth, "Zum Problem des Bazars (suq, çarşi)," *Der Islam* 51–52 (1974–1975), and "Villes islamiques, villes arabes, villes orientales? Une problématique face au changement," in A. Bouhdiba and D. Chevallier, eds., *La ville arabe dans l'Islam* (Tunis, 1982). Quotation, p. 198.

19. E. W. Burgess, "The Growth of the City," in R. E. Park and E. W. Burgess, eds., *The City* (Chicago, 1925).

20. H. Hoyt, *The Structure and Growth of Residential Neighborhoods in American Cities* (Washington, 1939).

21. C. D. Harris and E. L. Ullman, "The Nature of Cities," *Ann. Am. Acad. Pol. Sci.* 242 (1945).

22. A. Raymond, "Remarques sur la voirie des grandes villes arabes."

23. See E. Wirth, publications already mentioned (note 18), and "Die orientalische Stadt," *Saeculum* 26 (1975).

24. Robert Brunschvig, "Urbanisme médiéval et droit musulman," *REI* (1947).

25. See note 16.

26. Galal H. El-Nahal, *The Judicial Administration of Ottoman Egypt in the Seventeenth Century* (Minneapolis and Chicago, 1979).

27. Jacques Berque, "Médinas, villeneuves et bidonvilles," in *Maghreb. Histoire et sociétés* (SNED–Duculot, 1974); A. Sekaly, "Le problème des waqfs en Egypte," *REI* (1929).

28. André Raymond, "Les grands waqfs et l'organisation de l'espace urbain à Alep et au Caire à l'époque ottomane (XVIe–XVIIe siècles), *Bulletin d'Etudes Orientales (BEO)* 31 (1979). I shall mention these problems again in chapter 2, paragraphs 2.2.1 (Aleppo) (see ill. 7), and 4.4 (Cairo).

CHAPTER TWO

City Centers

The strong contrast between the central (public) and the private (residential) areas is, as we have seen, a traditional feature of the spatial organization of Arab cities. During the Ottoman era the development of the economic role of the towns, and the proliferation of commercial structures in their centers, resulted in an accentuation of urban "centrality" to the advantage of commercial activities.

1. THE SHIFTING OF THE SEAT OF POLITICAL POWER OUT OF THE CENTERS

1.1. A Traditional Feature

The shifting of the seat of political and military power away from the city center was a traditional feature of Arab cities. It is enough to mention the examples of Cairo and Damascus, with the establishment, during the Ayyubiḍ era, of the Citadel outside the city (Cairo) or on its outskirts (Damascus) to show that this was an ancient phenomenon, the consequences of which were significant for urban organization: the *taḥt al-Qalʿa* (under-the-Citadel) quarters rapidly became secondary commercial centers to which many activities were moved. J. Sauvaget made a masterful analysis of this transferal of the horse market (the *sūq al-ḫayl*) and the markets supporting the ruling and military groups (arms, transport, grain, etc.) and of the setting up of esplanades *(mīdān)* for training and parades. This wish to isolate the political center was just as marked in North Africa, as evidenced in the creation of Fez Ǧadīd in Morocco, or in the organization of the Qaṣba (Citadel), by the Hafsids, in Tunis, into a veritable small city, controlling the capital from a distance.[1]

1.2. Modern Examples

This phenomenon may also be observed during the Ottoman era and can be attributed to the same kinds of motivation:

- essentially the wish to ensure the security of the political center by isolating it from the agitation of the city, especially dangerous in times of crisis;
- the desire to separate the ruling class (which remained largely foreign) from the native subject population;
- practical considerations such as the difficulty of installing the army in an overpopulated urban center where communications were difficult (it was no doubt for this reason that, in Cairo, the urban police of the *wālī* [prefect] settled immediately to the south of the Fatimid city, beyond Bāb Zuwayla), and the need to have vast spaces available for the quartering of the troops and for their maneuvers.

Under these circumstances, this separation of the center of political and military power from the economic center was logically maintained where it already existed (e.g., in Cairo and Damascus), and a removal took place in other cities. In Baghdad the Ottoman pasha settled into a Citadel situated to the northwest of the town. In Mosul, where the center of authority, under the Mongols, was located not far from the Great Mosque, in the middle of the town (Ḥiṣn), the Turks built their "inside" Citadel (Iç Qalʿa) on the outskirts of the city, along the Tigris, near the boat bridge: isolated by a ditch on the edge of the town, the Citadel remained a place for quartering the army [M. L 20].[2] In Tunis the Muradites installed the governmental palace on the westerly limits of the city: the Dār al-Bey was perhaps constructed by Yūsuf Dey (1610–1637) [T. J 5]; it was extended by the Muradite Ḥammūda Pasha. But the Husaynite rulers no doubt found it still too close to the suq area, and from Ḥusayn bin ʿAlī on (1705–1740) they installed themselves at some distance from Tunis, in their residence of the Bardo, which was to remain the official city until the nineteenth century.[3]

Algiers was, for a long time, an exception to this segregation of the political center. The deys resided in the very heart of the city in the palace of the Ǧanīna [AL. F 7], a vast complex of buildings that housed the official residence, with the hall of the *dīwān* (council) and the private apartments of the ruler, of which the two palaces of Dār Aḥmad and Dār ʿAzīza are the only remains since the destruction of the Ǧanīna during the fire of 1844. Most political bodies were located close to the Ǧanīna: the Dār al-Sikka (the mint), Bayt al-Māl (financial administration), the post of the Būlukbāšī (the principal officers of the Turkish militia), and the main judicial courts. The barracks of the Janissaries themselves were dispersed in the lower part of the town of Algiers, not far from the palace. It was only in 1817, at the very end of Ottoman administration in Algeria, that the dey ʿAlī Ḫūǧa decided to transfer the seat of political power to the Qaṣba, located at the limit of the town that it dominated and controlled [AL. C 2]. There were probably at least two reasons for this move: the ruler's wish to evade the control of the militia, whose "revolutions" made and unmade deys; and also, no doubt, a desire to abandon a position that was too exposed to external dangers (the whole region of the Ǧanīna had been ravaged by the bombardment by Lord Exmouth and Van Cappellen's squadron in August 1816).[4]

From this point of view, Aleppo, with its Citadel and the sarāy(government center) located in the heart of the city, in close proximity to the suqs [A. P 16], made an exception that can no doubt be explained by the strongly defensive character of the Qalʿa, which spared the pashas the necessity of looking for a safer residence elsewhere.

Conversely, the importance of the role played by both the judges *(qāḍī)* and the courts *(maḥākim)* in the organization of the provinces and the everyday life of the subjects generally justified a very central location, in the immediate vicinity of the city markets. In any case, the links were so close between the courts of law and the main mosques, where they often sat or of which they formed annexes, that the *bayt al-qāḍī* was generally located in a very central situation, as the examples of Algiers, Cairo, Mosul, or Baghdad show so clearly.

2. THE URBAN CENTER

2.1. Economic Activities

The city center was mainly (and in many cases, exclusively) devoted to economic activity. I attempted to show earlier how the constitution of the Ottoman Empire had brought about an economic expansion that, in the main cities, gave rise to a spectacular development of the commercial centers. In a few cities where the situation prior to 1516 is known with some accuracy, this development can be assessed with precision. This, in particular, is the case of Cairo and Aleppo. In Cairo, at the time of Maqrīzī (the Egyptian historian of the fifteenth century), there were 87 markets (suqs) and 57 caravanserais. During the Ottoman era, the figures are 145 for the markets and 360 for the caravanserais. The major part of this commercial equipment was concentrated in the center of the Fatimid town (Qāhira) on both sides of the Qaṣaba [C. GH 5–6]. This zone of maximum activity covered approximately 32 hectares at the beginning of the fifteenth century, when there were to be found there 51 suqs (59% of the total) and 47 caravanserais (82% of the total). During the Ottoman era, a zone of 58 hectares, spreading around the Qaṣaba, the Ǧamāliyya, and the Marǧūš contained 58 suqs (out of 144 located suqs, or 40%) and 230 caravanserais (out of 348, or 66%).[5] In Aleppo the surface area of the economic center (called Madīna, or "City") can be estimated, thanks to the maps of J. Sauvaget, at

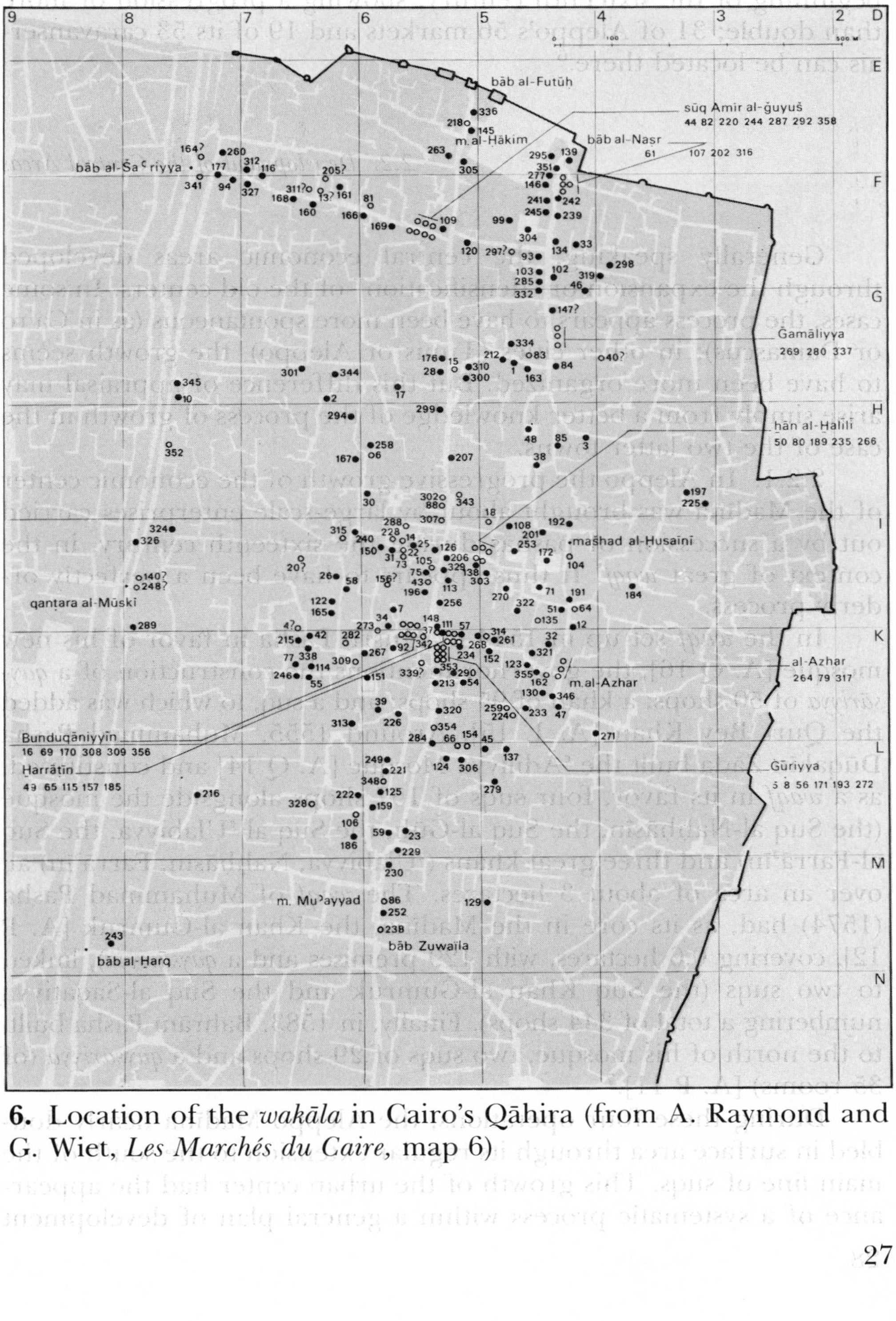

bāb al-Futūḥ
sūq Amīr al-ǧuyuš
44 82 220 244 287 292 358
m. al-Ḥākim
bāb al-Naṣr
61
107 202 316
bāb al-Šaᶜriyya
Ǧamāliyya
269 280 337
ḫān al-Ḫalīlī
50 80 189 235 266
mašhad al-Ḥusainī
qanṭara al-Mūskī
al-Azhar
264 79 317
m. al-Azhar
Bunduqāniyyīn
16 69 170 308 309 356
Ḥarrātīn
49 65 115 157 185
Ġūriyya
5 8 56 171 193 272
m. Muᵓayyad
bāb Zuwaila
bāb al-Ḫarq

6. Location of the *wakāla* in Cairo's Qāhira (from A. Raymond and G. Wiet, *Les Marchés du Caire,* map 6)

10.6 hectares during the Ottoman era, as against 5 hectares at the beginning of the sixteenth century, showing a progression of more than double; 31 of Aleppo's 56 markets and 19 of its 53 caravanserais can be located there.[6]

2.2. Development of the Central Areas

Generally speaking, the central economic areas developed through the expansion or "densification" of the old centers. In some cases, the process appears to have been more spontaneous (as in Cairo or Damascus); in other cities (Tunis or Aleppo), the growth seems to have been more organized. But this difference of appraisal may arise simply from a better knowledge of the process of growth in the case of the two latter towns.

2.2.1. In Aleppo the progressive growth of the economic center of the Madīna was brought about by large-scale enterprises carried out by a succession of pashas during the sixteenth century, in the context of great *waqf*. It thus appears to have been a perfectly orderly process.

In the *waqf* set up in 1544 by Ḫusrū Pasha in favor of his new mosque [A. Q 16], the governor mentions the construction of a *qaysāriyya* of 50 shops; a khan of 95 shops; and a suq, to which was added the Qurt Bey Khan [A. L 15]. Around 1555, Muḥammad Pasha Dūqakīn Zāda built the ʿĀdiliyya Mosque [A. Q 14] and constituted, as a *waqf* in its favor, four suqs of 157 shops alongside the mosque (the Suq al-Naḥḥāsīn, the Suq al-Ǧūḫ, the Suq al-ʿUlabiyya, the Suq al-Farrāʾīn) and three great khans (ʿUlabiyya, Naḥḥāsīn, Farrāʾīn) all over an area of about 3 hectares. The *waqf* of Muḥammad Pasha (1574) had, as its core in the Madīna, the Khan al-Ǧumruk [A. P 12], covering 0.6 hectares, with 129 premises and a *qaysāriyya*), linked to two suqs (the Suq Khan al-Ǧumruk and the Suq al-Saqaṭiyya numbering a total of 344 shops). Finally, in 1583, Bahrām Pasha built, to the north of his mosque, two suqs of 29 shops and a *qaysāriyya* (of 35 rooms) [A. P 11].[7]

During these four operations, the Aleppo Madīna nearly doubled in surface area through its regular extension to the south of the main line of suqs. This growth of the urban center had the appearance of a systematic process within a general plan of development

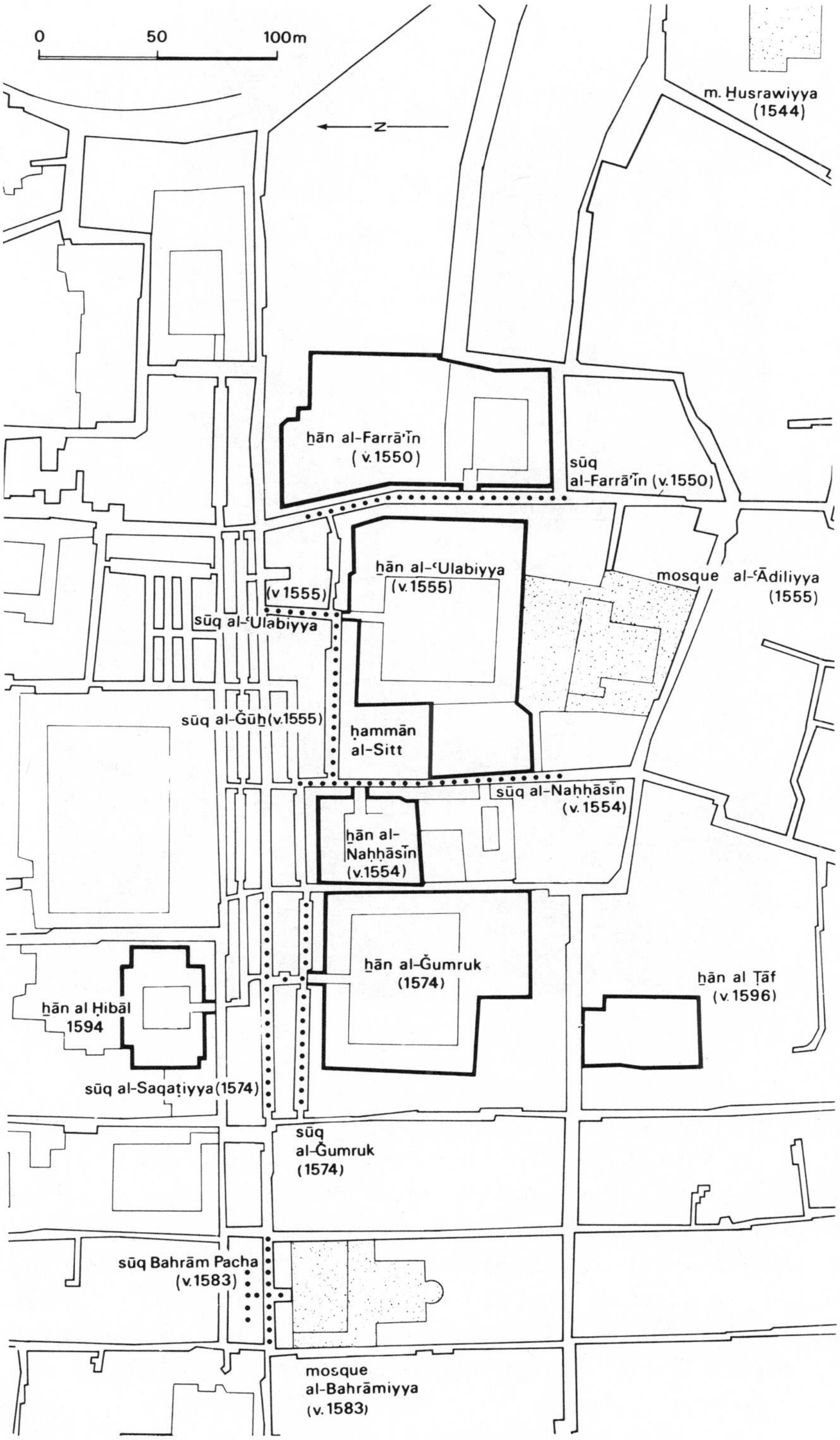

0
50
100m
N
m. Ḫusrawiyya
(1544)
ḫān al-Farrā'īn
(v.1550)
sūq
al-Farrā'īn (v.1550)
ḫān al-ʿUlabiyya
(v.1555)
(v.1555)
sūq al-ʿUlabiyya
mosque al-ʿĀdiliyya
(1555)
sūq al-Ǧūḫ (v.1555)
ḥammān
al-Sitt
sūq al-Naḥḥāsīn
(v.1554)
ḫān al-
Naḥḥāsīn
(v.1554)
ḫān al-Ǧumruk
(1574)
ḫān al Ṭāf
(v.1596)
ḫān al Ḥibāl
1594
sūq al-Saqaṭiyya (1574)
sūq
al-Ǧumruk
(1574)
sūq Bahrām Pacha
(v.1583)
mosque
al-Bahrāmiyya
(v.1583)

7. Extension of Aleppo's Madīna (16th century)

شعبة البريد

8. Khan al-Ǧumruk (Aleppo)

(one reason being that it had, as its framework, the very regular street structure of central Aleppo). In this case, the successive *waqf* builders, in their quest for still vacant sites, regularly transferred the center of their enterprises toward the west, each *waqf* being organized at the western limits of the previous one, thus following a progression that was perfectly logical but no doubt not really planned.

2.2.2. We are also fairly well acquainted with the operations carried out in Tunis during the seventeenth century because they benefited from the patronage of the Muradite emirs who governed the country during most of this period. The Suq al-Truk [T. J 6], the Suq al-Birka, the Suq al-Ǧarāba (Yūsuf Dey, before 1637), the Suq al-Kabābǧiyya, and the two great markets of makers and sellers of caps (the Suq al-Šawwāšiyya), all constructed by the Muradites, reshaped the town center over an area of 1.2 hectares in the zone situated near the Great Mosque, where the Muradites had built their most significant monuments: the Mosque of Yūsuf Dey (1611), the Mosque of Ḥammūda Pasha (1655), the Dār al-Bey (before 1659), the school (Madrasa) Murādiyya (1673). In this case, the patronage of the emirs progressively developed a region that had remained open to the west of the Hafsid suqs so thoroughly that the saturation of the economic center of Tunis around the Zaytūna Mosque subsequently brought the Husaynite beys to locate their own creations in relatively outlying zones: the Suq al-Sakkāǧīn (Ḥusayn bin ʿAlī), the Suq al-Balāṭ, the Suq al-Blaġǧiyya (1756–1757), the Suq al-Kutubiyyīn (between 1758 and 1782), and the Suq al-Bey (1804).

The lacunae in our information (which arise essentially from insufficient knowledge of extant sources) do not allow us to say whether an impetus from the center of the empire gave rise to, or at least encouraged, local initiatives. It is not impossible that the Ottoman government had taken, in this regard, more positive action than has generally been supposed. Only a thorough perusal of the imperial correspondence *(awāmir sulṭāniyya)* could enlighten us on this point.[8]

2.3. The Case of Mosul

In one case only can a complete transfer of the market zone be noted during the Ottoman era. In Mosul, which presents the rather exceptional case of a round city, the urban center during the Mongol era was situated in the vicinity of the central Great Mosque [M. O 13]. After the Ottoman conquest, the center of economic activity shifted to the southeast, so that during the eighteenth century the suq area made up a triangular sector widening from the Ṣāġa toward the river Tigris [M. N 19]. Two reasons can explain such an exceptional process: on the one hand, the installation of the Citadel along the Tigris no doubt prompted the development of a commercial area of the *taḥt al-Qalʿa* (under-the-Citadel) type; on the other hand, the proximity to the crossing place over the Tigris by a temporary or fixed bridge was equally likely to encourage the installation of suqs and caravanserais linked to the movement of trade.

2.4. Urban Dissymmetry

Though the economic district effectively represented the nucleus of the city, the evolution of the cities (in particular, their growth) during the Ottoman era resulted inevitably in "anomalies" in the ideal layout of concentric circles, which was rarely perfectly achieved. The most frequent outcome of the unequal development of a city was a marked "decentering" of the economic core, especially when urban expansion was realized through the formation of suburbs.

2.4.1. The most characteristic example of this urban dissymmetry may be found in Cairo. Until the end of the Mamluk period, the area of the Qaṣaba had occupied the central part of the city (which did not then extend much beyond Fatimid Qāhira). The development of the southern quarter (which began during the Ayyubid era because of the attraction exerted by the Citadel and by the proximity to Old Cairo) and the creation of a veritable western quarter beyond the Canal (Ḫalīğ), along the main axes leading to Būlāq and the Nile, contrasted with the stagnation in the east and in the north, and resulted in the decentering of the formerly central cell of the city. Growth toward the east, limited in any case by the natural obstacle formed by the cliff of the Muqaṭṭam mountain, was made difficult by the existence of cemeteries (much developed during the Mamluk era) and by the presence of a zone of tells (hills) resulting from the accumulation, over the centuries, of earth, refuse, and dirt brought from inside Cairo, along the eastern fortified wall of the city. Similarly, to the north, in a zone that had apparently experienced great expansion during the Mamluk era,[9] the suburb of Ḥusayniyya knew only limited development. Thus, in 1798, Qāhira, the core of Cairo, occupied the northeast quarter of the city.

2.4.2. In Aleppo the development of two important suburbs, noticeable as early as the Mamluk era along the main commercial routes toward the north (Anatolia), the northeast, and the east (Iraq and Persia), produced the same results. In the eighteenth-century town, the "City" developed in a comparatively decentered position to the west of the Citadel, the presence of the river Quwayq, not far from the western wall of the town, having very likely limited the development of suburbs in this direction. In the same way, the center of Damascus was decentered by the extension of the southerly suburbs of the Mīdān along the pilgrimage route. As previously mentioned, the shifting of the economic center of Mosul toward the southeast placed it on the outskirts of the town.

2.4.3. It is really only in Algiers and Tunis that the functional centrality of the city corresponds to a visible topographical reality, for reasons that are, moreover, quite different. Established as early as the sixteenth century in a setting that would not change until 1830 and that is profoundly marked by the nature of the site (with limits imposed upon it by mountain and sea), Algiers experienced no development of suburbs either to the north or to the south and kept its rather balanced shape. Tunis's expansion was equally restricted by the geographical limitations of its site (a cliff to the west, a lagoon to the east); beginning in the medieval period, it spread into two suburbs, in the north (Bāb Suwayqa) and in the south (Bāb Ǧazīra), the simultaneous development of which ensured the geographical equilibrium of the city.

3. ORGANIZATION OF THE URBAN CENTERS

The organization of the urban centers conforms to a logical pattern that is perfectly readable on the map, although it is difficult to say whether it is the result of deliberate action on the part of the authorities (imperial or local) or of a "natural" evolution in which economic factors are responsible for a sort of spontaneous selection and localization of activities.

3.1. The Bedestan

The central location of the Ṣāga (market for currency exchange), whose role was essential in international trade, and its customary proximity to the Great Mosque, have already been noted: there are no exceptions to this situation. It brought with it, in many cases, the central location of the Jewish quarter.

It is more difficult to reach a conclusion about the role of the *bedestan*. The works of H. Inalcik and K. Kreiser have brought to light the interest of the imperial authorities in the development of *bedestan,* structures where international trade was concentrated, which explains their diffusion in most of the main centers of Rumelia.[10] As regards the Arab cities, the question of the *bedestan* remains somewhat uncertain. It is true that the existence of *bedestan* is attested in numerous provincial capitals, notably Algiers, Cairo, Damascus, and Aleppo. But we are not sure that, in all these cases, this kind of commercial structure was systematically built by the Ottomans to form the center of the suq quarter. The function of the *bedestan* corresponds exactly to that of the *qaysāriyya* mentioned in Fez and Baghdad, well before the Ottoman era. It was a zone of variable size (in some cases a part of a street, in others a whole district) in which concentrated merchants whose activities concerned precious goods (e.g., cloth merchants); for this reason, it was was usually closed at night. The *qaysāriyya* of Fez, as described by Leon the African, was "a sort of small town surrounded by walls" with twelve gates, where most varied trades were assembled in the very center of the city; that of Tlemcen is said to have looked, as early as the fourteenth century, like an "international concession" reserved for the activities of European merchants.[11] This market of luxury goods (in Algiers both booty and slaves were traded there)[12] no doubt often took the name of *bedestan* in reference to similar commercial centers that had been installed in Anatolian and Balkan cities during the fifteenth and sixteenth centuries. Similarly, in Cairo, the Khan al-Ḫalīlī is sometimes called Bāzastān, though its architectural organization was completed before the Ottoman conquest.

But it is equally true that the *bedestan* of Algiers (where there also existed a *qaysāriyya*) was created a little before 1563;[13] and in Syria *waqf* documents mention the successive construction of two *bedestan* in the commercial center of Damascus. The old *bedestan* (Bedestan al-Qadīm), built by Murād Pasha toward 1595, afterward became a suq. Before 1608, Murād Pasha constructed a *bazzāzistān* (or *bāzistān*). Its description obviously calls to mind the *bedestan* mentioned by H. Inalcik: it was a monument covered by 9 domes, with 12 windows, 4 doors, consisting of 61 shops, intended for cloth merchants, with a shop reserved for the shaykh al-Bazzāzīn [D. E 3].[14] We are not absolutely certain of the exact location of this monu-

9. Khan al-Ḫalīlī (Cairo) (from R. Hay)

ment, and it is therefore impossible to find a material representation of the precise description given by the *waqf* document.[15]

3.2. Suq Network

The economic center was normally organized around that section of the markets where important business was carried out. In many cases, it was a street that thus served as the main axis of the city, as one can see in Algiers (along the road leading from the urban center to Bāb Ğazīra and to Bāb ʿAzzūn), in Cairo (on both sides of the Qaṣaba, the main street since the Fatimid era), or in Aleppo (where the main line of suqs linking Bāb Anṭākiyya to the Citadel ran along the southern side of the Great Mosque).

In other towns, the suqs formed networks whose regularity may sometimes be attributed to the Greco-Roman origins of the street design. This is certain for Damascus, where the main market developed along streets perpendicular to the street of the Suq al-Barīd leading to the Great Mosque (on the site of an ancient temple) to the north, and to the big straight suq (the Roman *decumanus*) to the south. But in Baghdad, a purely Arab creation, this grid plan is also quite apparent in the zone of the big markets and caravanserais. This central zone was opened widely toward the exterior of the town through a number of main axes along which the transit of individuals and goods took place, and which were very often the starting point for the development of suburbs; this evolution is obvious in Cairo and Aleppo.

3.3. Tunis, Aleppo, and Mosul

The fairly regular character of this layout, starting from the theoretical center of the commercial quarter, appears very clearly on the plans of most big Arab cities (e.g., in the cases of Tunis, Aleppo, and Mosul).

• In Tunis the suq quarter is organized around the Great Mosque [T. J 6–7] with so perfect a regularity that ancient origins seem more than probable. Slightly apart from this central zone, one finds the *funduq,* intended for the storage of goods and for the lodging of merchants.

• In Aleppo the suq sector develops following an axis that occupies the line of the ancient street, the Great Mosque here taking the place of the earlier temple or church. Caravanserais (khan) of particularly imposing dimensions are constructed on the outskirts of the central zone [A. P 12].

• In Mosul, in a center that developed during the Ottoman era, the structure is just as obvious and just as logical. The most specialized elements, the *qaysāriyya,* occupy a central position in the suq triangle: the caravanserais are located in a more peripheral position [M. N 19].

4. ELEMENTS COMPOSING THE URBAN CENTER: SHOPS AND MARKETS

The basic element of the urban center was the shop, the gathering of which constituted the suq (market).

4.1. Shops

The shops *(dukkān* or *ḥānūt)* were simple in structure and thus easily and cheaply built, which made them remarkably adaptable according to need: *waqf* documents sometimes mention hundreds of these constructions, built to be used for the religious foundations. The shops of Cairo described by Lane were little different from those of Fez studied by Le Tourneau, and one finds the same type, with minor changes, as far as Iraq: the premises were small and square, 5 to 6 feet high, 3 or 4 feet wide, sometimes extended by a storage room (eventually situated above the shop); the flooring was usually raised 2 or 3 feet above ground level and was frequently extended into the street by a bench *(maṣṭaba);* the stall was closed at night by two or three horizontal shutters; the top shutter could form an awning, and the lower ones could be folded back to serve as a counter, a display stand, or a divan. The shopkeeper's lodgings and his main storeroom *(ḥāṣil)* were normally situated elsewhere. The extension of these shops over hundreds of meters formed the trading center of the city. There were probably over 20,000 of them in Cairo, and Damascus had approximately 6,600.[16]

4.2. Markets

The market (suq) was generally an open structure. In the central regions of the city it followed strict technical specialization, with each trade occupying a determined and usually permanent part of

10. Shops in a street of Cairo (from E. W. Lane)

urban space. Since some trades were more or less monopolized by certain communities, this specialization could also have an ethnic or a religious character. This stability of the market zone as a whole must not make one overlook changes in detail due to very diverse reasons: the appearance of new products and trades (e.g., coffee, to-

11. Market in Cairo's Qaṣaba (from D. Roberts)

bacco, and the trades derived from them); the decline of certain activities (which resulted in a move away from the center); or in some cases technical considerations, as in Cairo where the *bārūdiyya* (gunpowder sellers) moved away from the center after the accidents that occurred there in 1671 and 1703.

4.3. "Spontaneous" Markets

In a great number of cases, the suq was but a double row of shops built along a street. The development of the markets was thus carried out by a transformation of residential streets into streets of predominantly commercial activity, an evolution that was easily made owing to the simplicity of the basic unit, the shop. In this way, during the Ottoman era, main centers flourished and developed; secondary centers appeared along the more commercial streets; and new markets sprang up in the vicinity of the town gates and inside the new suburbs that expanded outside the walled city. The suqs of the Bānqūsā region in Aleppo [A. J 23], of the Mīdān in Damascus [D. D 8], of the Marǧūš [C. F 7], and the region beyond Bāb Šaʿriyya in Cairo, and that of the street of Bāb ʿAzzūn in Algiers [AL. B 8] are typical examples of these "spontaneous" markets.

4.4. Architectural Realizations

But our period is also rich in planned operations that assumed real architectural character, above all, naturally, when the development of the markets affected the area closest to the urban center, near the Great Mosque. Building enterprises of this kind often had a religious objective; for example, when the new suqs were created to finance the maintenance of pious monuments or foundations. But they were also, obviously, political operations that were to contribute toward enhancing the prestige of the founder, prince, or other notable. Thus the care with which these economic enterprises were sometimes architecturally linked to the religious or utilitarian structures that they complemented.

I have already mentioned the series of covered suqs that were built in the vicinity of the Great Mosque of Tunis by the Muradite beys, and in particular by Yūsuf Dey, between 1610 and 1637. The most typical of these markets, the Suq al-Truk [T. J 6], consists of a paved and vaulted street and of a double range of shops separated by columns, painted green and red in the Turkish fashion. In the middle of the suq one comes upon a cafe, one of the few (and one of the oldest) that remain from the Ottoman era. The Suq al-

12. Muradite suqs in Tunis

Birka [T. K 5], where slaves were sold, is centered in a small covered square, decorated with six columns, from which radiate the four streets that compose the market.

In Aleppo the great *waqf* operations launched by the pashas of the sixteenth century in the southern part of the Madīna comprised a series of suqs, some of which have real architectural character and are indeed structurally connected, by systems of vaults and domes, to the main *waqf* buildings. This is the case, for example, of the Suq Khan al-Ǧumruk [A. P 12] and of the Suq al-Saqaṭiyya, built in 1574, and linked to the gateway of the fine Khan al-Ǧumruk; or again of the suq of Bahrām Pasha [A. P 11] that adjoins to the north the mosque built in 1583, the connection between them being provided

13. Entrance of Khan al-Ǧumruk (Aleppo)

for by a system of three domes, above the monumental entrance to the mosque, and above the entrance of the *qaysāriyya,* which is also included in the *waqf.*[17]

In Cairo, finally, the big covered suq called Qaṣaba Riḍwān is the central part of a set of buildings that make up the *waqf* founded by the emir Riḍwān Bey between 1629 and 1647 [C. N 6].[18] The Qaṣaba Riḍwān where shoemakers *(qawwāfīn)* were gathered is 125 meters long. For fifty meters, the street is covered by a ceiling of wood pierced with square openings. On either side of the six-meter-wide street, on the ground level, the western and eastern facades are built of stone, and large apertures allow for the development of commercial structures (retailers' shops). Strong consoles support the projecting upper floor, pierced with alternately simple or double rectangular openings: a *wakāla* and a *rab*ᶜ (collective building) are to be found at that level. The only covered suq remaining in Cairo, the Qaṣaba of Riḍwān Bey is the most impressive building of its kind that Cairo has preserved from its thousand-year-old history.

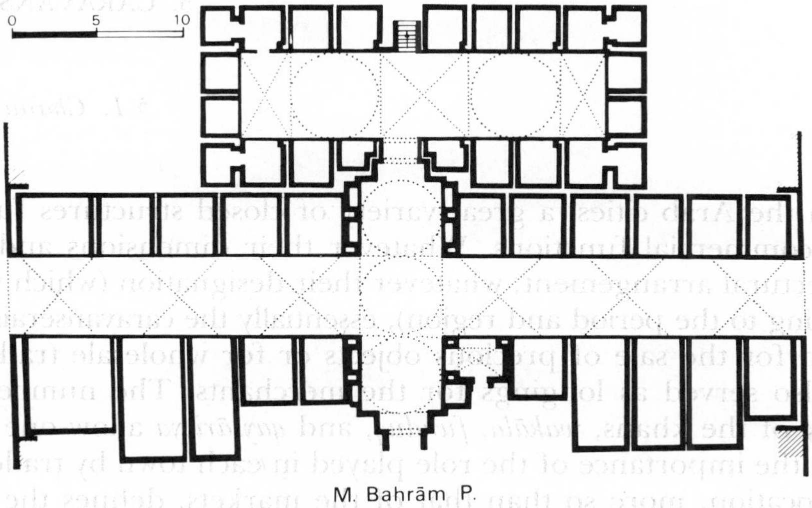
0
5
10
M. Bahrām P.

14. Suq Bahrām Pasha in Aleppo (from J. Sauvaget)

15. Qaṣaba Riḍwān in Cairo

5. CARAVANSERAIS

5.1. *Characteristics*

In the Arab cities, a great variety of closed structures fulfilled other commercial functions. Whatever their dimensions and their architectural arrangement, whatever their designation (which varied according to the period and region), essentially the caravanserais were utilized for the sale of precious objects or for wholesale trade, but they also served as lodgings for the merchants. The number and density of the khans, *wakāla, funduq,* and *qaysāriyya* allow one to establish the importance of the role played in each town by trade; and their location, more so than that of the markets, defines the limits of the "business center," the "Madīna/City."

The caravanserais were often specialized in the trade of a single product, which in many cases accounted for their name, as, for instance, in Cairo, the Wakāla al-Ṣābūn, where soap was traded [C. F 5]. Very frequently, the authorities intervened to enforce the monopoly enjoyed by these establishments in a determined commercial sector, a monopoly that allowed the administration easier control over trading and facilitated the redistribution of goods by the merchants. Therefore, caravanserais were often used by merchants of the same ethnic origin who had nearly exclusive rights to the trade of a given product. The Palestinian merchants in the Wakāla al-Ṣābūn thus controlled the sale of soap in Cairo.

This continuity in the use of the caravanserais explains why, in spite of a quite varied terminology, the architectural structure of these buildings remained relatively the same, the greatest variable being the dimensions, which were in keeping with the commercial activity of each center. Whatever the importance of the building, it is, in every case, centered around a courtyard (sometimes covered), and it generally comprises rooms on the ground floor for storing goods and apartments upstairs for the merchants' lodgings.

5.2. *North Africa*

In North Africa the caravanserais, termed *funduq* or *wakāla* (locally, *ukala),* were buildings of usually modest importance, which corresponded to the secondary role played by the Maghrib in Mediterranean trade. We know little about the *funduq* of Algiers. They disappeared along with the other central buildings of the town after the conquest. We assume, however, that their architectural structure, their use (trade and lodging), even their number (scarcely more than 20 or so) can be compared with those of Tunis, of which, on the contrary, a good number have survived down to our day. The most typical, and one of the best preserved in Tunis, is the *funduq* that was built in 1660 for the French trading community ("Nation") on a model that was extremely common in Tunis under the Muradites and the Husaynites [T. G 10]. It is a functional building, devoid of any artistic pretensions. A vaulted entrance leads to a square courtyard surrounded by a portico of 16 columns with a number of stores built in vault-covered rooms. On the upper floor, lodgings open

16. Funduq of the French "Nation" in Tunis

on to a gallery. In all, it is a building of approximately 1,000 square meters, containing about 50 rooms. It was completed by a second, more or less similar, building, the "Nation" and the Consulate sharing the use of both buildings.[19] The al-ᶜAṭṭārīn Funduq, situated in the very center of the suqs [T. I 7], is built on an exactly identical model, but on an even smaller scale (a square 25 meters wide). The caravanserais (khan) of Mosul seem to have resembled this type of monument, of little architectural value and of modest dimensions. This, at least, is the impression given by the ones that remain of the 35 that the town probably possessed during the Ottoman era, with their open courtyard *(sāḥa),* their stores and stables on the ground floor, and their one or more upper floors *(ṭābiq).*[20]

5.3. Cairo, Aleppo, and Damascus

Quite different in their architectural scope and artistic ambition were the big caravanserais of the main commercial capitals of the empire: Cairo, Aleppo, Damascus, and probably Baghdad. The very number of buildings identified for the Ottoman period in these cities clearly indicates this change of scale: some 60 khans in Damascus and in Aleppo, 360 *wakāla* in Cairo. Their size, which in some cases exceeded half a hectare, and their architectural quality are also indicative of the magnitude of the commercial movement that produced them.

5.3.1. The basic structure of the *wakāla* of Cairo was fixed well before the beginning of the sixteenth century, as is shown by the Wakāla of Q̱āytbāy in Bāb al-Naṣr (1480, no. 9 in the list of classified monuments), or by the Wakāla al-Ġūrī (1504–1505, no. 64). It would hardly change during the Ottoman era, except for the size of the buildings and a few details (decoration, conception of the gateways). Two buildings dating from the seventeenth century, and still existing today, are good examples of this type of monument in Cairo. The Wakāla of Ḏūlfiqār Katḫudā (built in 1673) [C. G 5] is in a very damaged state today, but the fine drawings of Pascal Coste give us a precise picture of the monument in its original state: a monumental angled entrance opening at the crossing between Ǧamāliyya and Tumbakšiyya streets gives access to a vast courtyard with, in its center, an oratory and a fountain. The dimensions of the building proper

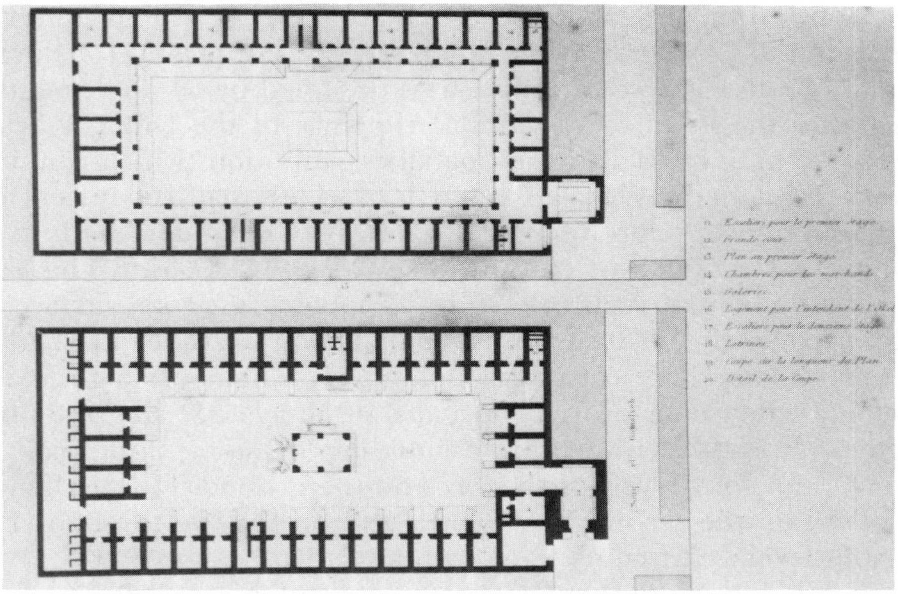

17. Wakāla of Ḏūlfiqār Katẖudā in Cairo (from P. Coste)

18. Wakāla of Ḏūlfiqār Katẖudā in Cairo (from P. Coste)

are 75 by 35 meters (about 2,600 square meters). The ground floor, according to Coste's drawing, comprised 32 storerooms for the merchants' goods. The second floor was occupied by 34 apartments *(ṭabaqa)* and the third by a *rabᶜ*.[21] If the style of the Ḏūlfiqār Wakāla has something "Syrian" in its spatial organization (which is more or less horizontal), the Wakāla Bāzarᶜa, located less than 100 meters away, and roughly contemporaneous, is typically "Egyptian," with its verticality that reminds us of the Ġūrī Wakāla [C. G 5].[22] The *wakāla* forms an irregular rectangle 25 by 45 meters (the total surface area is approximately 1,000 square meters). The fine facade, adorned with *mašrabiyya* (wooden projecting openings) is four floors high. A monumental gateway leads to a courtyard of an average size of 27 by 12 meters. It is surrounded by a building of stone and brick constructed on four levels, with stores on the ground floor, lodgings in a gallery on the second floor, and a *rabᶜ* on the two top floors, with 19 split-level apartments, each with a terrace.

5.3.2 The monumental caravanserais of Aleppo also reveal the strength of local traditions: the Mamluk Khans al-Ṣābūn (built by Ouzdamour) and al-Abrak are fine examples of an architecture that obviously inspired the plan and decoration of Ottoman buildings. The

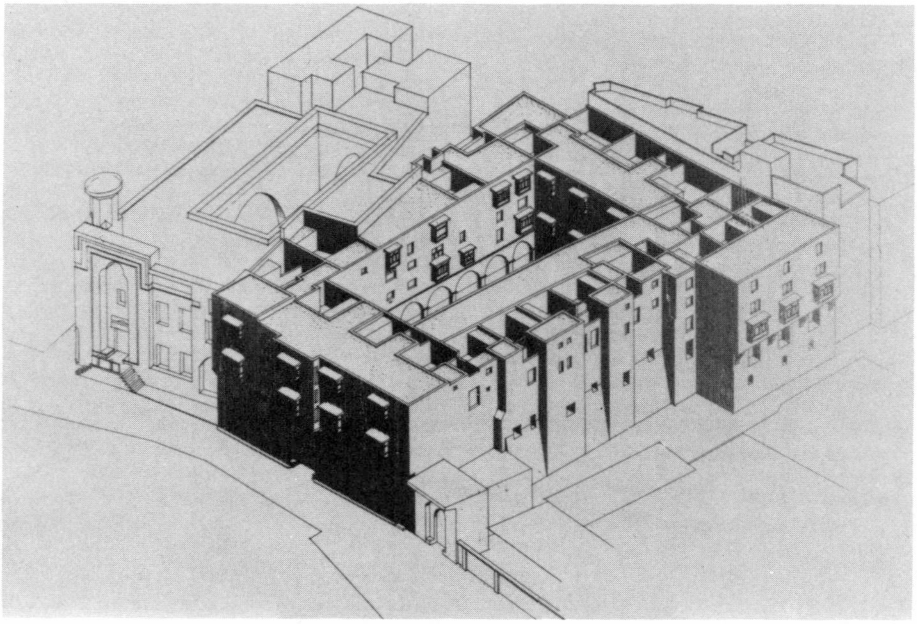

19. Wakāla Bāzarᶜa in Cairo: restoration proposal (from F. Aalund)

20. Facade of the Wakāla Bāzarʿa

Qurt Bey Khan (built around 1540) [A. L 15] is remarkable for its scale (2,500 square meters) and for the monumental nature of its entrance, which is preceded by a small suq for the use of its occupants. The central basin and the great *īwān* are very typical of this "Syrian" architecture. The Khan al-Ǧumruk [A. P 12], constructed around 1574, is of exceptional size (52 shops on the ground floor, 77 rooms above, a surface of about 6,400 square meters); its deco-

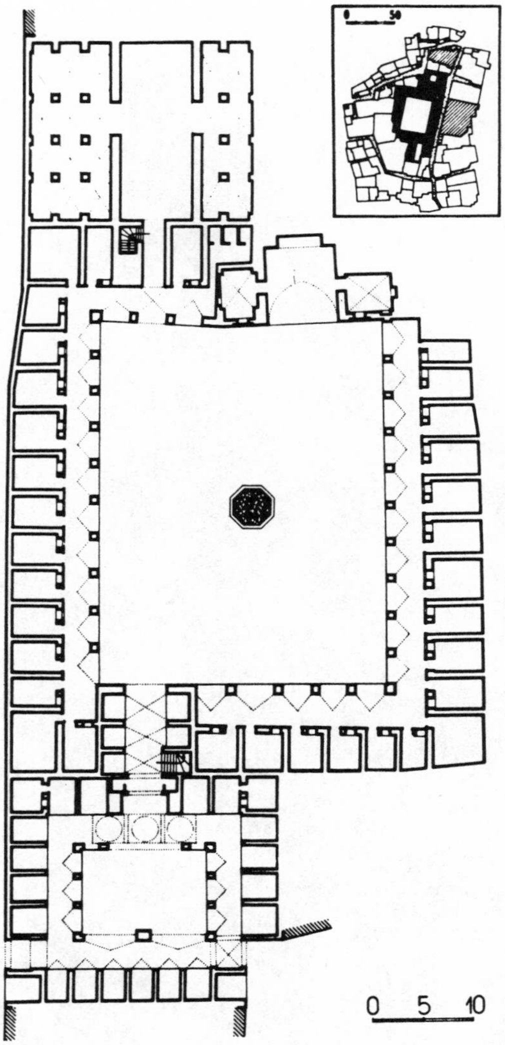
0 50
0 5 10

21. Qurt Bey Khan in Aleppo (from J. Sauvaget)

ration plainly reminds one of Mamluk antecedents and very subtly links the caravanserai with the suqs that were built at the same time, in the context of the *waqf* of Muḥammad Pasha. Much later than these two sixteenth-century caravanserais, the Khan al-Wazīr (1682) is an example of the lasting influence of Mamluk art; this is particularly perceptible in the decor of the main and the interior facades, in this case the Syrian traditions visibly dominating the influence of Istanbul [A. N 15].[23]

22. Courtyard of Qurt Bey Khan

5.3.3. In comparison with this stability of traditional types in Tunis, Cairo, or Aleppo, the appearance of a new model of khan in Damascus, in the eighteenth century, is a remarkable phenomenon. Caravanserais covered by a system of domes were not new in Damascus: we have seen that the *bedestan* built before 1608 by Murād Pasha included nine domes, possibly an "Ottoman" layout, perfectly explicable in this case, since the construction of a *bedestan* in a provincial capital could refer only to models already existing in the capital of the empire. The adoption of domed roofing seems to have had great success at the beginning of the eighteenth century, as is indicated by the examples of the Khan Sulaymān Pasha al-ᶜAẓm (built in 1732, two domes); the Khan Safarğalanī (built before 1757, three domes); or the Khan Sidraniyya (built before 1757, two domes). But the Khan Asᶜad Pasha expresses a particularly noticeable "Ottoman" influence in the layout of its vast courtyard (27 meters wide), with its four pillars supporting nine great domes, an architectural feature that is unprecedented in Damascus and has no equivalent in Aleppo [D. F 5]. The building of such an imposing structure was certainly justified by the commercial activity of Damascus at that period and

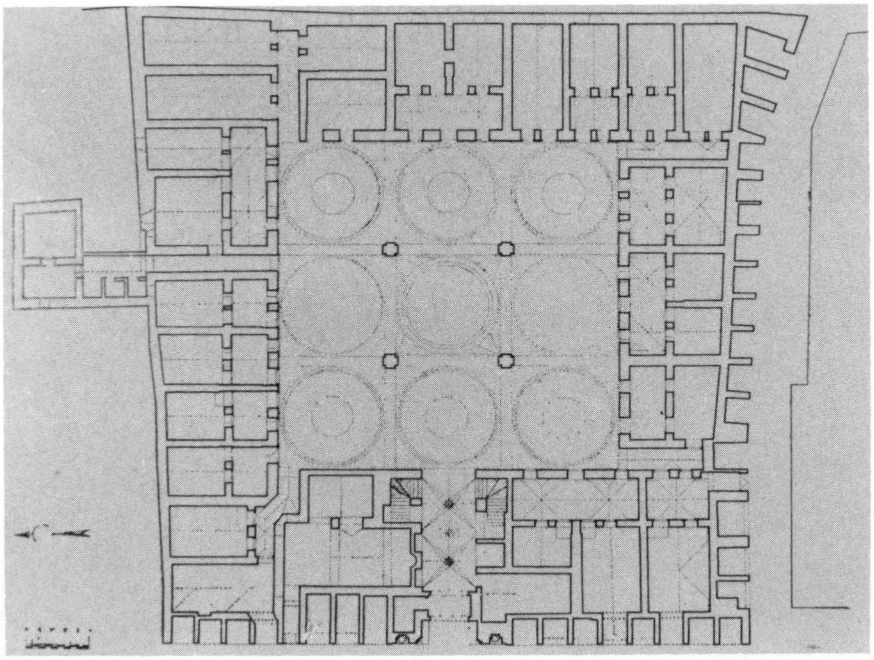

23. Khan Asʿad Pasha in Damascus (from A. Rīḥāwī)

by the pasha's wish to ensure revenues for the great *waqf* he was setting up; but one can also suppose that it was considered as an enterprise of prestige that was to enhance the authority of the local ruler. In these circumstances, the very style of the building, so evidently evocative of constructions in the capital, is not to be dismissed as a secondary element.[24]

In this case, as in all those that have been mentioned previously, the erection of purely commercial buildings (suqs or caravanserais) took on obvious political significance; even when it was only implicit, it was no doubt just as real as in the case of the nonutilitarian buildings that shall be mentioned later on.

Notes

1. Marcel Clerget, *Le Caire,* 2 vols. (Cairo, 1934), I, 144–146; Jean Sauvaget, "Esquisse d'une histoire de la ville de Damas," *Revue des Etudes Islamiques (REI)* (1934), 464–465, and *Alep. Essai sur le développement d'une grande ville syrienne, des origines au milieu du XIXe siècle,* 2 vols. (Paris, 1941), 169–170; Roger Le Tourneau, *Les villes musulmanes de l'Afrique du Nord* (Algiers, 1957), 12–13; Robert Brunschvig, *La Berbérie orientale sous les Ḥafṣides,* 2 vols. (Paris, 1940–1947), I, 342–344.

2. Saʿīd Dīwağī, "Qalʿa al-Mawṣil," *Sumer* 10, no. 1 (1954).

3. Jacques Revault, *Palais et demeures de Tunis,* 4 vols. (Tunis, 1967–1978), I, 41, 323; Slimane Mostafa Zbiss, *Monuments musulmans d'époque Husseynite en Tunisie* (Tunis, 1955).

4. Pierre Boyer, *La vie quotidienne à Alger à la veille de l'intervention Française* (Paris, 1963), 63; André Raymond, "Le centre d'Alger en 1830," *Revue de l'Occident Musulman et de la Méditerranée* 31, no. 1 (1981).

5. André Raymond and Gaston Wiet, *Les marchés du Caire* (Cairo, 1979).

6. J. Sauvaget, *Alep,* Album, plans LXII and LXX.

7. André Raymond, "Les grands waqfs et l'organisation de l'espace urbain à Alep et au Caire a l'époque ottomane (XVIe–XVIIe siècles)," *Bulletin d' Etudes Orientales (BEO)* 31 (1979), 114–117.

8. Research in progress about Aleppo by Jean-Pierre Thieck.

9. See Doris Behrens-Abouseif, "The North-Eastern Extensions of Cairo under the Mamluks," *Annales Islamologiques* 17 (1981).

10. Halil Inalcik, "The Hub of the City: The Bedestan of Istanbul," *International Journal of Turkish Studies* 1, no. 1 (1979–1980); K. Kreiser, "Bedesten–Bauten in Osmanischen Reich," *Istanbuler Mitteilungen* 29 (1979).

11. Jean-Léon l'Africain, *Description de l'Afrique,* A. Epaulard, ed., 2 vols. (Paris, 1956), I, 198; Roger Le Tourneau, *Fès avant le Protectorat* (Casablanca, 1949), 375–376; Charles Brosselard, "Les inscriptions arabes de Tlemcen," *Revue Africaine* 4 (1860), 5 (1861), 6 (1862).

12. Jean-Michel Venture de Paradis, "Alger au XVIIIème siècle," *Revue Africaine* 41, no. 114; Paul Eudel, *L'Orfèvrerie algérienne et tunisienne* (Algiers, 1902), 76–77.

13. Albert Devoulx, *Les édifices religieux de l'ancien Alger* (Algiers, 1870), 140.

14. Jean-Paul Pascual, *Damas à la fin du XVIe siècle* (Damascus, 1983), 108–115. See also Fouad Yahia, "Inventaire archéologique des caravansérails de Damas," thesis, University of Provence, 1979, 378.

15. J.-P. Pascual, *Damas,* thinks that the *bazzāzistān* was located where the Khan al-Ǧumruk stands now. This khan is covered with domes, but its L shape suggests no resemblance to the *bedestan* [D. E 4].

16. Edward W. Lane, *Manners and Customs of the Modern Egyptians,* rev. ed. (London, 1954), 321–324; André Raymond, *Artisans et commerçants au Caire au XVIIIème siècle,* 2 vols. (Damascus, 1974), I. 268–272; R. Le Tourneau, *Fès,* 315–316.

17. J. Sauvaget, *Alep,* 215–217.

18. Edmond Pauty, *Les Palais et les maisons d'époque musulmane au Caire* (Cairo, 1933), 81–82; A. Raymond, "Les grands waqfs," 121.

19. J. Revault, *Palais,* I, 27; II, 396.

20. Hashim al-Genabi, *Inner Structure of the Old City of Mosul* (Mosul, 1981).

21. A. Raymond, *Artisans,* I, 257; Pascal Coste, *Architecture arabe* (Paris, 1839), pls. XLIII, XLIV, p. 40.

22. Flemming Aalund, "The wakalat Bazarʿa," in M. Meinecke, ed., *Islamic Cairo, Art and Archaeology Research Papers (AARP)* (London, 1980).

23. J. Sauvaget, *Alep,* 215, 216, 264; "Inventaire des monuments musulmans de la ville d'Alep," *REI* (1931), 97, 101; Heinz Gaube, *Arabische Inschriften aus Syrien* (Beirut, 1978), 21.

24. ʿAbd al-Qādir al-Rīḥāwī, "H̱ānāt madīna Dimašq," *Annales Archéologiques Arabes Syriennes* 25 (1975), 64–69.

CHAPTER THREE

Residential Districts

1. INTRODUCTION

If the study of the central commercial districts can be supported by abundant and precise documentation, that of the residential districts comes up against difficulties of both documentary and methodological character.

1.1. Problems of Method

One can obtain accurate knowledge of the residential districts in Arab towns only from a thorough perusal of archives; in particular, this enables us to establish a link between the socioeconomic status of the town inhabitants and the character of their residence. This study is possible owing to the inexhaustible sources constituted by the court documents *(maḥākim)* on successions that provide, in some cases, information on the profession, the economic status, and the place of residence of the deceased. This kind of research has just begun; until now, it has been carried out systematically only for Cairo, a situation that does not allow for comparisons that would be absolutely necessary. For the time being, we cannot totally rule out the possibility that the Egyptian case is wholly exceptional. For this reason, researchers, who depend on very general information supplied by local chronicles or accounts of travelers, have generally tended to underestimate socioeconomic factors with respect to residences.

Another negative element in this area is the fact that archaeological research provides only partial and, in a way, misleading information. Generally speaking, still existing monuments are those of the rich. The situation is the same for a large part of the *waqf* documents, which are used more and more by researchers. We are thus informed only about the characteristics of the residence of the more well-to-do strata of the population, mainly the ruling class and the native bourgeoisie. This is the case of the truly remarkable research carried out successfully, for the last twenty years, in Tunis and Cairo, but that can be used only for a limited part of the population.[1] Ignoring this limitation may expose a researcher to serious misinterpretation.[2] Recently launched research on the middle-class house from remains and from *waqf* and law court documents will no doubt partly make up for the present one-sidedness of these conclusions.[3] It is to be feared, however, that our knowledge of ordinary housing will remain very incomplete through lack of architectural evidence (the poorer habitat necessarily being very fragile) and of archive documents (which mostly concern transactions about important properties). This is a most regrettable situation, since this habitat naturally concerned the greater part of the urban population.

These deficiencies have resulted in an overshadowing of the importance of material factors in residence location in classical Arab cities, while our everyday experience shows that money is the decisive element in the geographical distribution of urban lodging. The particular character of the most often used documentation, legal deeds about sale of property registered in the courts, has contributed to this overshadowing: the documents we use mention global prices concerning *construction* but give absolutely no precise indication about the value of the land itself (a decisive variable in understanding urban phenomena); they also lack any indication concerning dimensions and surface areas, which are vital information if one is to carry out a study of the differential value of urban land according to the district and the importance of the construction.

Our incomplete knowledge of sources, and the deficiencies of our information, partly explain why various generally accepted ideas on the Arab town have been maintained even in otherwise excellent recent studies. Among the more questionable stereotypes in this area, the following are to be mentioned:

• First is the idea that traditional urban Arab society was comparatively egalitarian, though recent research has proved exactly the contrary. I would like to recall that in Cairo during the Ottoman era the ratio of the lowest to the highest succession noted in the *Maḥkama* registers was 1 to 60,000.[4] The corollary resulting from the previously mentioned illusion is that the Arab town, in its organization, rejected any segregation founded on socioeconomic factors. One may quote what the late A. Abdel Nour wrote on the subject: "Traditionally, it was the rule in the Arab towns that rich and poor families were neighbours . . . there existed no real distinction [in Aleppo] between the richer and the poorer districts."[5]

• Second is the idea that the traditional Arab house was, as a rule, individual, closed to the exterior, turned inward on itself, not only so as to ensure the isolation of family life but, more than this, to fulfill a religious conception of life, the home structure being the expression of a global perception of the universe and of the place of man in this universe. On this point, one could give a number of references. I will merely quote again A. Abdel Nour: "The home, closed to the outside world, on the contrary opens wide onto the courtyard, and from there, to the sky; the courtyard (celestial, as our texts put it so well) thus carries out the communication, not with other men, but with the universe."[6]

None of these assertions can be accepted as being totally valid. A close study of Arab towns reveals an impressive collection of facts that contradict them and that cannot simply be dismissed as being aberrant or untypical.

2. LOCALIZATION OF RESIDENTIAL DISTRICTS

2.1. Principles of Localization

The fundamental phenomenon remains the marked centralization of commercial activities. To a certain extent, residential areas were located in relation to the central quarter of the suqs, as they attracted the native population, largely made up of craftsmen and tradesmen, and repelled the ruling class, which needed space that was difficult to find in a zone monopolized by commercially oriented structures, markets, or caravanserais.

Craftsmen and shopkeepers did not usually live in their workshops or shops, as these did not normally include domestic premises and did not generally give direct access to the building they were attached to. Consequently, the suqs were empty at night and were often closed and guarded.[7] Once his work day was over, the merchant or craftsman went home. To make this daily "commuting" easier, they tried to live as close as possible to the market where they worked. In Cairo, during the eighteenth century, the average distance between the place of residence and the place of work was generally little more than 500 meters, a few minutes' walk.

The scarcity of land in the town center, plus the concentration of economic structures, hindered the development of poorer dwellings in the vicinity of the suqs. The underprivileged part of the population was thus forced out to the town outskirts. Conversely, members of the more well-to-do categories of the population, merchants, but also shaykhs who wished to be fairly close to the mosque-university, had the financial means to put up residences (sometimes palaces) near the center. The interaction of these factors resulted in a layout in successive rings, with the wealthiest part of the population residing near the center, and the poorer part residing some distance away.

However, resorting to collective housing with a more intensive exploitation of usable space made it possible to solve the already mentioned contradiction between the attraction of the central areas and the difficulty of finding available room for building at moderate cost. We shall see later on how this collective habitat developed, either by using the caravanserais, or (at least in Cairo) by using collective buildings (the *rab*ᶜ).

Another factor that modified this system of localization was the attraction, for the richest part of the population, of districts well away from the center, where space was available in abundance and where the wealthy could build large residences, allowing them to lodge important retinues of followers and servants and to lay out gardens. In this way, there developed luxurious residential areas inhabited by the native bourgeoisie or by members of the ruling class, on the outskirts of the cities, where poorer districts could also be found.

As spatial organization evolved under the influence of socioeconomic factors, geographical regrouping developed to meet the community requirements of religious or national minorities. This tendency, which was very ancient, could only be encouraged by the strengthening of a community system like that of the *millet* during the Ottoman era. It is not surprising, then, that in all big Arab cities there appeared quarters of predominantly religious character grouping "protected" Christian and Jewish communities *(ḏimmī):* Ḥāra al-Naṣārā for the Christians, Ḥāra al-Yahūd for the Jews. It was also the case for Muslim minorities (the Alaouite districts of Antioch, the Shi'ite district of Baghdad), or ethnic groups (the Kurdish districts of Damascus, Aleppo, or Baghdad; the Andalusian districts of Algiers or Tunis). The motives for these regroupings are obvious: the desire to reinforce the cohesion of religious or national groups so as to facilitate the fulfillment of religious or cultural aspirations; the concern to ensure the security of groups isolated by their language, their religion, or their traditions; the authorities' will to control them more closely. These groups were so well defined geographically that one can map them accurately in all big Arab cities. The most extreme cases are those of Antioch, with its 45 districts divided into two large Christian zones (split up into Armenians and Greeks) and two large Alaouite zones, separated by the zone of Turkish quarters (27 quarters situated in the heart of the city);[8] and that of Jerusalem with its 18 *ḥāra* divided into four big zones: Christian (8 quarters of Greeks, Latins, Copts), Armenian (4 quarters), Muslim (4 quarters), and Jewish (2 quarters).[9] From this point of view, it is obvious that Ottoman rule favored the partitioning of big cities, and did so until the very end of the period. Cairo is a typical example of this evolution, with the progressive setting up, during the last decades of the

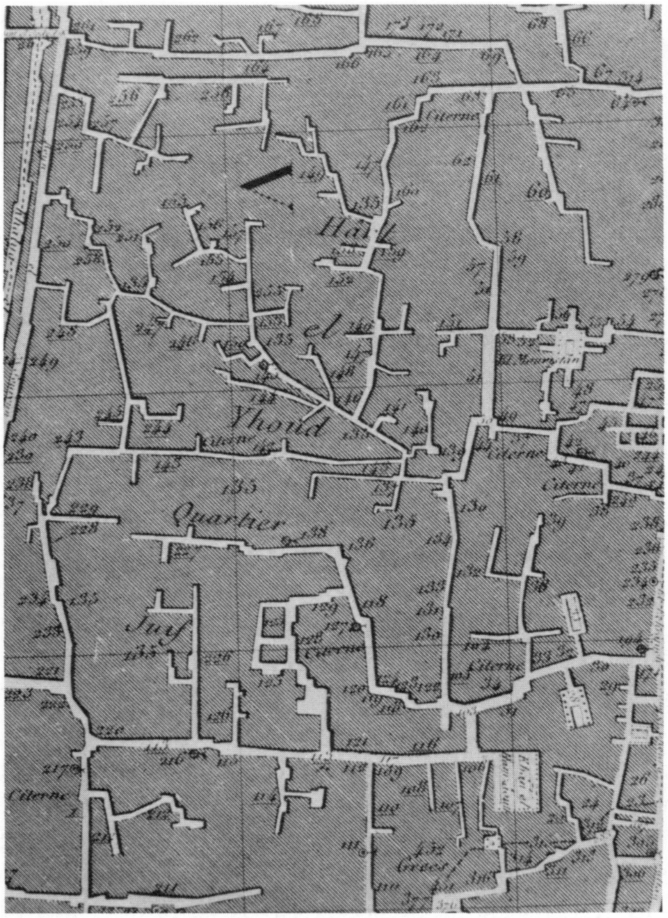

Quartier
Juif
el
Yhoud

24. Ḥāra al-Yahūd in Cairo (from the *Description de l'Egypte*)

eighteenth century, of a district of Latin rite Syrian Christians, whose settlement in large numbers in Egypt went back no further than 1730, and whose organization into an autonomous community was even more recent [C. G 9].[10]

2.2. Examples of the Localization of Dwelling Districts

2.2.1. Jacques Revault's remarkable studies on Tunis show how the area close to the commercial center was "colonized" during the Ottoman era by the fine houses of the people belonging to the high society: dignitaries of the ruling class (the "Makhzen"); *ʿulamā* (members of the religious institution, mainly grouped around the Zaytūna Mosque); and rich merchants, of the native bourgeoisie.[11] The progressive congestion of the area situated immediately around and to the south of the central zone explains the installation, during the eighteenth century, and especially during the nineteenth century, of new palaces in the northern part of the Madīna, an area where, until then, more modest habitats had dominated. The Madīna proper, being, on the whole, reserved for specialized commercial activities and for the residence of the elite and the middle classes, it was therefore in the suburbs *(rabāḍ)* that people of humble background, especially newcomers, countryfolk *(barrānī),* and foreigners, lived. The southern suburb of Bāb Ǧazīra mainly accommodated people from the south; the northern suburb of Bāb Suwayqa was chosen by people from the north, rural immigrants tending naturally to settle down close to the road leading to their home places.[12]

This spontaneous sorting of the population is particularly apparent in the case of one of the last elements to arrive in Tunis, the Andalusians, whose last (and most important) immigration dates back to 1609. The aristocracy of the Morisques settled inside the Madīna in the chic districts, where a street was to be named after them (Street of the Andalusians), and where sumptuous residences convey to us the memory of the prosperity and power of the Lakhoua and the Beji families [T. M 7]. At the same time a much humbler district developed outside the Madīna, between Bāb Suwayqa [T. A 3] and Bāb Qarṭaǧinna, [T. D 10] on a site occupied by Spanish immigrants as early as the thirteenth century. This district, which took the name of Bīǧa (Spanish: Vega), developed along Trunǧa Street, near the Subḥān Allāh Mosque and the Madrasa al-Andalusiyya, both monuments probably built during the first three decades of the seventeenth century.[13] In this case, the socioeconomic characteristics of the Andalusians proved to be more powerful than the community of national origin, and they determined a partition following the hierarchy of wealth; the more prosperous part of the community merged with the local bourgeoisie, while the greater number constituted a national quarter in a popular district.

2.2.2. We have at our disposal for Cairo information that is both more accurate and more complete, owing to the indications supplied by the succession documents recorded in the *Maḥkama,* and to the topographical indications given by the *Description de l'Egypte.* For the

1776–1798 period, I have been able to locate the homes of 334 craftsmen and merchants, of which 179 were artisans and merchants who worked in Qāhira. Unfortunately, this information, by its very nature (successions), tends to underrepresent the poorer elements of the population while overrepresenting the middle class and the bourgeoisie.

Keeping this distortion in mind, one can describe the pattern of residence in Cairo as follows. In the area closest to the zone of maximum economic activity of the Qaṣaba lived a certain number of artisans and shopkeepers, many of whom inhabited flats in *rab*ᶜ and caravanserais. The zone that stretched from the central area of the big markets to the outlying area of the *ḥāra,* was the usual place of residence of the middle class, of the bourgeoisie of merchants, and of shaykhs connected with al-Azhar Mosque: a third of the shaykhs whose houses I was able to locate for the period 1774–1798 (22 out of 67) lived less than 200 meters away from the mosque-university.

An exception to this rule were those inhabitants of Cairo who had settled in more distant, but more spacious, districts along the Ḫalīǧ, in the "casins" (small houses) described by Pascal Coste, or around the Birka (lake) al-Azbakiyya [C. H 12], the most sought after district where many big merchants *(tuǧǧār)* had long taken up residence. The Šarāybī, a family of coffee *tuǧǧār,* had residences there that were luxurious enough for the ruling emir, Riḍwān Katḫudā,

25. The "casins" along the Ḫalīǧ in Cairo (from P. Coste)

to purchase them for himself, around 1750. And when, in 1776, fire destroyed the quarter of al-Sākit (C. I 13), wealthy merchants like ʿUmar Ġurāb, Aḥmad ʿAbd al-Salām, and Maḥmūd Muḥarram built fine houses there, on the western bank of the Azbakiyya.[14] A map indicating the location of the houses of the artisans and tradesmen working in the Ġūriyya area expresses this double characteristic with perfect clarity: a ring of residences close to the center, and a few residences farther away, beyond the Ḫalīǧ.

Near the outskirts of the town there developed popular districts that made up a continuous belt to the north and to the east of Qāhira; this localization corresponded roughly to the zone where more or less closed residential districts, or *ḥāra,* were to be found. "The quarters," writes the German traveler Niebuhr, "are commonly places of residence for artisans and other poor inhabitants who work . . . in little shops in the suq or in shopping streets."[15] This description is confirmed by the analysis of the *Maḥkama* successions: the residents of the *ḥāra* zones (57 cases noted between 1776 and 1798) left successions amounting to only 35.5% of the average for the whole of the population studied (40,943 paras as against 109,101 paras). It is in this zone of *ḥāra* that were to be found, for the most part, the *ḥawš,* a type of very poor habitat that I will discuss later on.

In the case of members of the Egyptian ruling caste, the segregation was even stricter. After the Ottoman conquest the emirs had abandoned Qāhira as a residential district, probably because of the development of commercial activities in that part of Cairo. During the seventeenth century, the palaces of the beys and officers were mainly grouped around the Birka al-Fīl [C. Q 9], which was, around 1700, the chic district, par excellence (40% of the residences of the emirs between 1650 and 1755), so much so that we have located no resident there during the seventeenth and eighteenth centuries who was not an emir. In the eighteenth century, the emirs progressively shifted their residences toward the region west of the city, as they were no doubt attracted by abundant green spaces and water, and as they were anxious to flee the dense and busy areas of the eastern part of Cairo. The Birka al-Azbakiyya, which had long been a place of residence for the local bourgeoisie, became, from 1750 on, one of the favorite districts of the ruling caste.[16] It was on the banks of this lake that Muḥammad Bey al-Alfī, one of the richest emirs of the time, built the palace that Bonaparte would occupy in 1798 and 1799 [C. H 13]. The emirs' desire to isolate themselves from the native

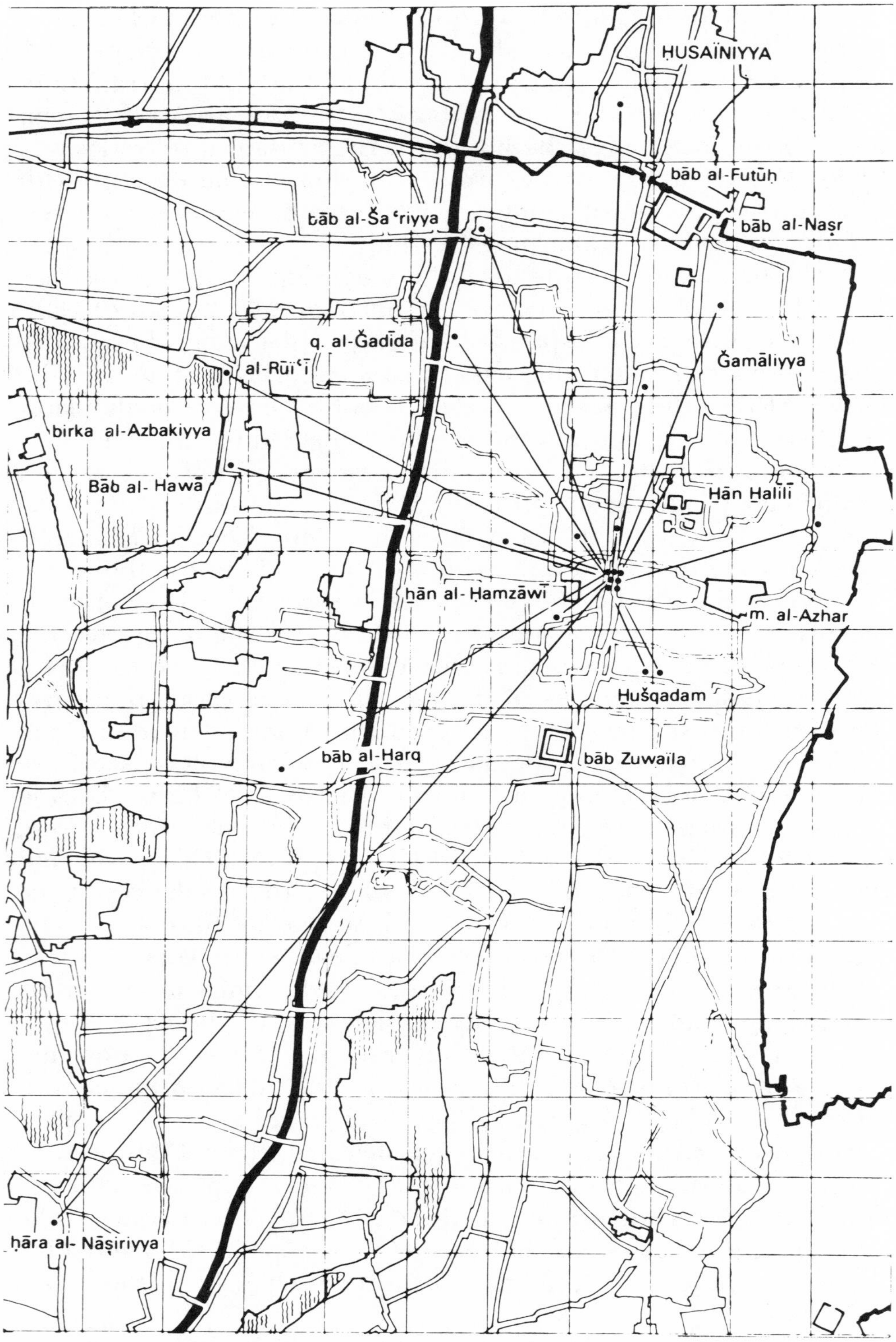
ḤUSAĪNIYYA
bāb al-Futūḥ
bāb al-Naṣr
bāb al-Šaʿriyya
q. al-Ğadīda
al-Rūīʿī
Ğamāliyya
birka al-Azbakiyya
Bāb al-Hawā
Ḫān Ḫalīlī
ḫān al-Ḥamzāwī
m. al-Azhar
Ḫušqadam
bāb al-Ḫarq
bāb Zuwaila
ḥāra al-Nāṣiriyya

26. Location of the houses of the Ġūriyya people in Cairo

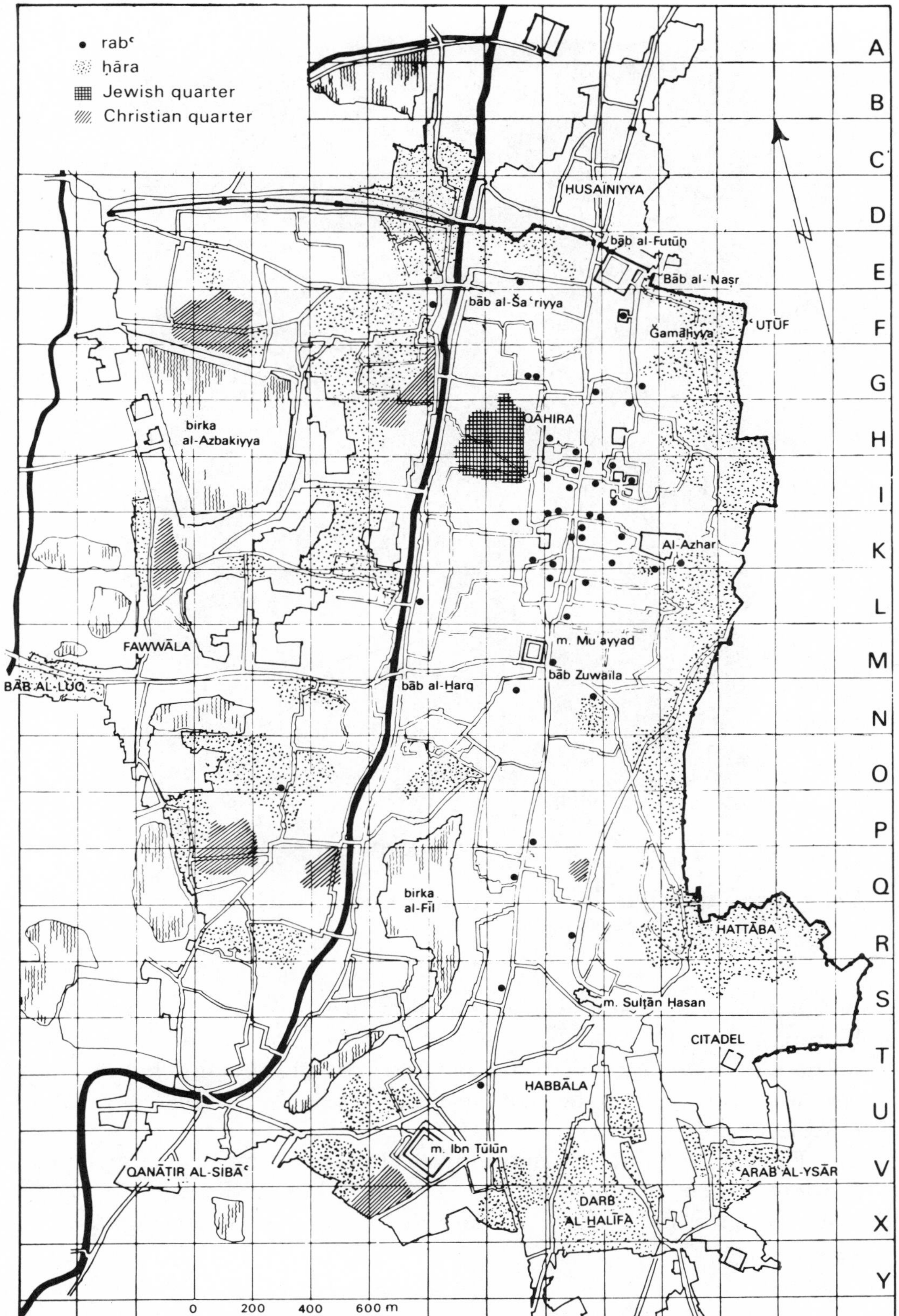

rab^c
ḥāra
Jewish quarter
Christian quarter
HUSAINIYYA
bāb al-Futūḥ
Bāb al-Naṣr
bāb al-Ša'riyya
Ǧamāliyya
'UṬŪF
QĀHIRA
birka
al-Azbakiyya
Al-Azhar
FAWWĀLA
m. Mu'ayyad
bāb Zuwaila
BĀB AL-LUQ
bāb al-Ḫarq
birka
al-Fīl
ḤAṬṬĀBA
m. Sulṭān Ḥasan
CITADEL
ḤABBĀLA
m. Ibn Ṭūlūn
QANĀṬIR AL-SIBĀ'
'ARAB AL-YSĀR
DARB
AL-ḪALĪFA
0 200 400 600 m
A B C D E F G H I K L M N O P Q R S T U V X Y Z
15 14 13 12 11 10 9 8 7 6 5 4 3 2 1

27. Location of *ḥāra* and *rab*ᶜ in Cairo

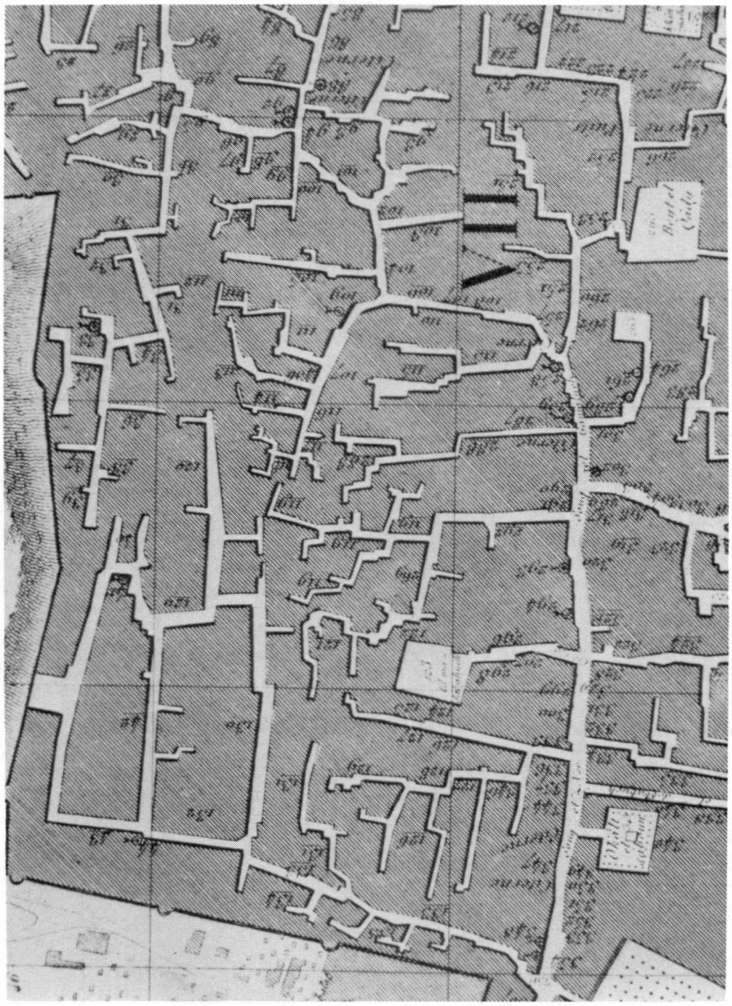

28. Closed quarters in the Ǧamāliyya area of Cairo (from the *Description de l'Egypte*)

population was expressed with open cynicism. When the same Muḥammad Bey al-Alfī had to pass from one to another of the palaces he had built outside Cairo, he avoided crossing the city, saying that "he was ashamed to be seen in the streets by shopkeepers and passer's-by."[17]

Finally, the minority communities (Jews and Copts) were grouped in their respective quarters (one Ḥāra al-Yahūd and seven Christian districts) with some rigor. As late as the middle of the eighteenth

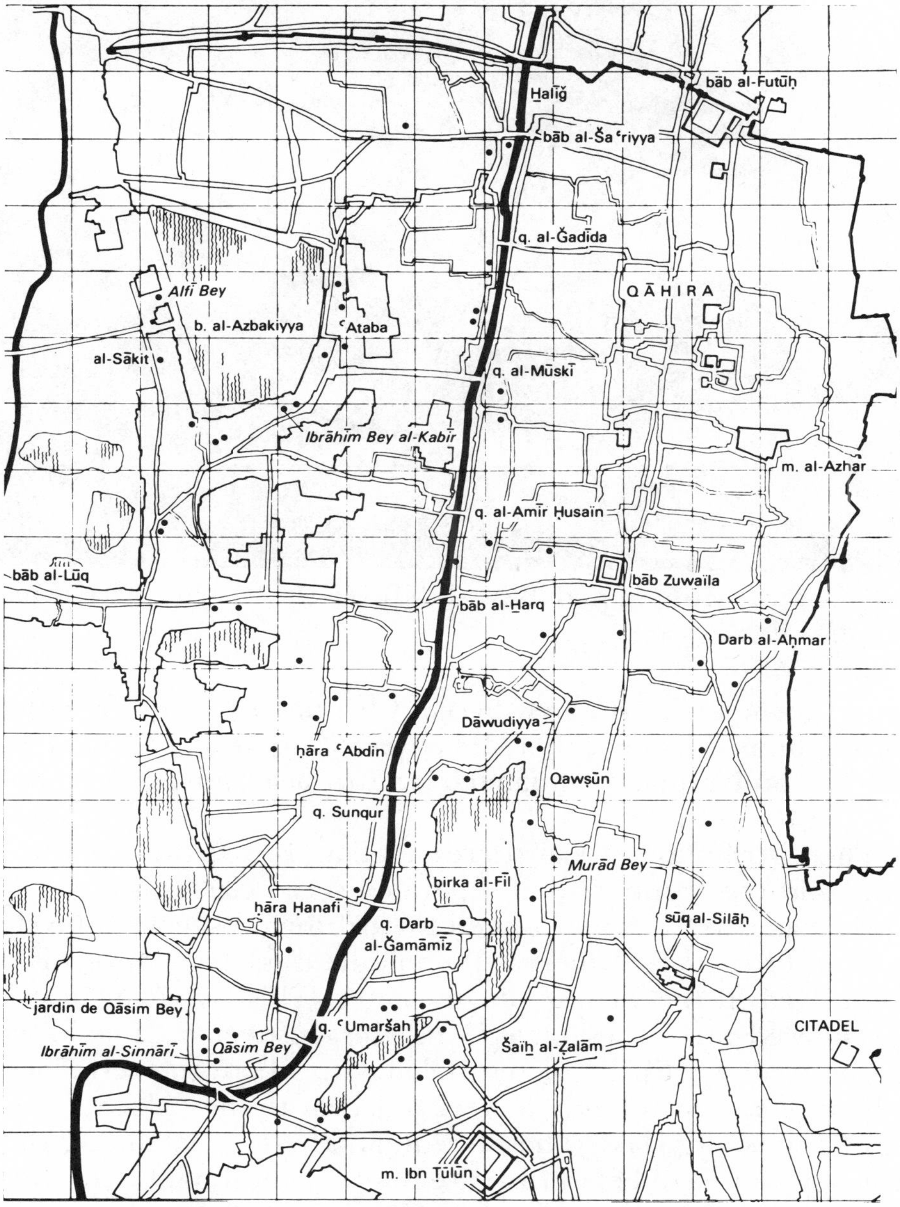
bāb al-Futūḥ
Ḫalīǧ
bāb al-Ša ͑riyya
q. al-Ǧadīda
QĀHIRA
Alfī Bey
b. al-Azbakiyya
ʿAtaba
al-Sākit
q. al-Mūskī
Ibrāhīm Bey al-Kabīr
m. al-Azhar
q. al-Amīr Ḥusaïn
bāb al-Lūq
bāb Zuwaïla
bāb al-Ḫarq
Darb al-Aḥmar
Dāwudiyya
ḥāra ʿAbdīn
Qawṣūn
q. Sunqur
Murād Bey
birka al-Fīl
ḥāra Ḥanafī
q. Darb al-Ǧamāmīz
sūq al-Silāḥ
jardin de Qāsim Bey
q. ʿUmaršah
CITADEL
Ibrāhīm al-Sinnārī
Qāsim Bey
Šaïḫ al-Zalām
m. Ibn Ṭūlūn

29. Residences of the emirs in Cairo, in 1798

30. Palace of Muḥammad Bey al-Alfī on the Azbakiyya (from the *Description de l'Egypte*)

century, members of the new Syrian Christian community settled in a well-delimited zone situated between a quarter of indigenous Christians and a quarter inhabited by Europeans on the left bank of the Ḫalīǧ [C. G 9].[18]

The distribution of Cairo's residential districts thus reproduced in the field the frontiers that separated social classes, the most underprivileged strata being pushed toward the outskirts of the city in the zones of the *ḥāra,* whereas the middle class and bourgeois population lived in the vicinity of the center. This layout in successive rings allowed for certain exceptions, the most remarkable of which was the dwelling district of the Azbakiyya, where the residences of the bourgeoisie of the *tuǧǧār* were adjacent to the palaces of members of the ruling class. The horizontal frontiers delimiting the social strata proved to be, in this case, more determinant than the vertical frontiers that separated the "foreign" ruling caste from the indigenous *raᶜya.* To a large extent, therefore, the structure of Cairo society showed up on the town plan, social or community divisions being accurately expressed through geographical localizations.

2.2.3. The work of J. C. David makes identical phenomena evident in Aleppo. The map of the different kinds of traditional habitat drawn up by this researcher clearly shows this layout of residences in successive rings.[19] The "bourgeois" houses (types III and IV in David's classification) were grouped on either side of the Madīna and the Citadel, near the commercial center of the town. Farther away there spread the zones of the middle-class habitat (types I and II). Very poor "semirural" habitats were characteristic of the outlying zones to the east and south of the city. The only notable exception to this distribution concerned a minority district, the Christian quarter of Ǧudayda, a "bourgeois" area that was located to the northwest of the town [A. F 11].

3. INDIVIDUAL AND COLLECTIVE HOUSING

3.1. The Individual House

The characteristics of so-called traditional Arab housing have been expounded so often that one naturally hesitates to set them forth once again.[20] The Arab house is supposed to fulfill, by its introverted character, the *social* aspirations of the Muslims and, by its vista toward a unitary beyond, their *religious* creed.

I do not claim to challenge the primacy of the individual habitat turned inward onto the courtyard, of which aerial photography or a cadastral map of any Arab city would evidently show the predominance. But I think it would be useful to offer a few cautionary remarks:

• As for the origins and character of this house with a central courtyard, one hardly needs to point out that its characteristics are Mediterranean, climatic and cultural reasons explaining its wide diffusion, while history enables one to trace back its permanence to the most remote antiquity. It is no doubt perfectly adapted to the comparative seclusion of family life in Muslim society, but it would naturally be going too far to make a purely religious interpretation of it.

• As for the description of this type of habitat, it is necessary to keep in mind the fact that most references concern a private archi-

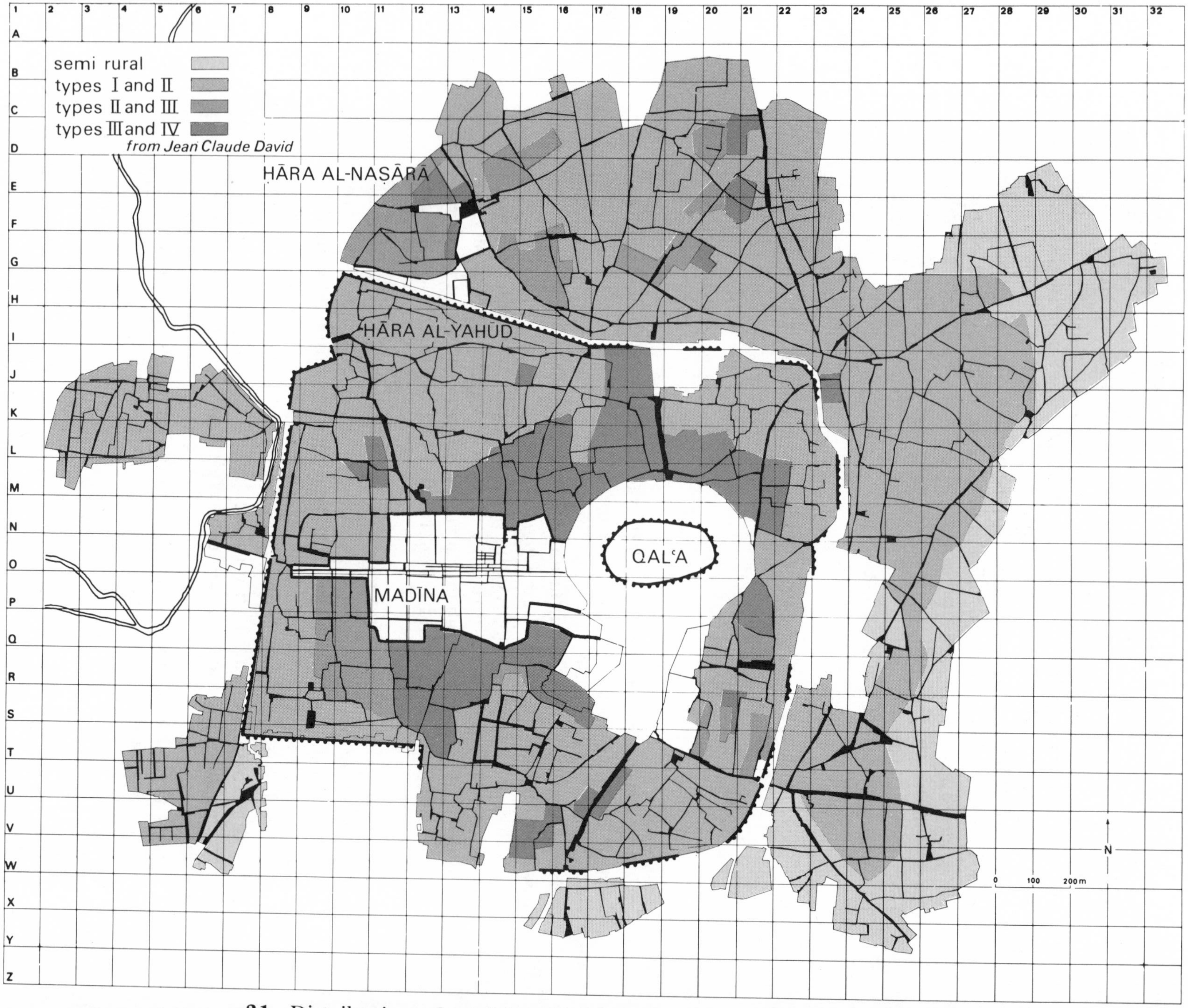
semi rural
types I and II
types II and III
types III and IV
from Jean Claude David
ḤĀRA AL-NAṢĀRĀ
ḤĀRA AL-YAHŪD
QALʿA
MADĪNA
N
0 100 200 m

31 Distribution of traditional habitats in Aleppo (from J. C. David)

tecture particular to the wealthiest class, the only one, in fact, for which we have sufficient archaeological documentation and historical information. Study of the dwellings of the lower middle classes, or poorer population, reveals different customs, which it would be exaggerated to label "atypical" just because thus far research has been directed mainly at a type of habitat that is only partly characteristic. It is to correct this viewpoint that I shall devote to these "atypical" phenomena an attention that is no doubt excessive if one considers the problem from a merely statistical point of view.

3.2. The Traditional Individual Habitat

The most striking characteristic that one notices when going from one province to another is the force of local traditions that perpetuated, until the end of the eighteenth century, fundamentally different ways of building, even when geographical proximity or the closeness of mutual relations could have resulted in reciprocal influences. On the other hand, the fact that all these countries were under common domination could have resulted in an evolution toward bringing together life-styles. In fact, the influence of the capital and of the prevailing culture conveyed by the thousands of military and administrative personnel who settled in provincial cities seems to have had an effect only in regard for construction details that sometimes did modify the decor, but not the basic organization, of the house.

3.2.1. There is obviously a similarity in the organization of domestic space in the Maghrib (Algeria and Tunisia). It is particularly noticeable in the importance of the hall *(sqīfa),* which played a significant social role in that it enabled the master of the house to entertain visitors without permitting them to enter the house itself. This explains the presence of benches placed in recesses in the lateral walls, and also the sometimes luxurious decoration, of marble marquetry or earthenware tiles. The central part of the house consists of a courtyard that, in Tunis, is often rectangular; the two long sides are devoid of galleries, the short sides only being lined with porticos; the main room, opposite the entrance, is extended by an alcove *qbou,* and this T-shaped room is the main ceremonial room in the house. The upper floor covers only a part of the ground floor. The courtyard of the Algerian house is a square, entirely surrounded by gal-

32. *Sqīfa* of Muṣṭafā Pasha's palace in Algiers

leries, which are to be found also on the second and third floors. If the Algerian house often developed vertically, it was perhaps because, in Algiers, space was particularly scarce, and because the uneveness of the ground did not favor spreading out horizontally.[21]

3.2.2. In the houses and palaces of Cairo, the architectural style inherited from the Mamluk period changed little until the eighteenth century, the Ottoman influence being limited to decorative contributions. A corridor led to a courtyard that was used only as a passageway and on to which opened, on the ground floor, open *(taḫtabuš),* or closed *(mandara)* reception rooms, and upstairs the ar-

33. Dār ʿUṯmān Dey in Tunis (beginning of the 17th century)

cades of an open loggia facing north *(maqʿad).* A large room spread out on the second floor inside the "harem" part of the house; this *qāʿa,* often luxuriously fitted out, was used, like the *mandara,* as a reception room. The development of balconied windows, equipped with *mašrabiyya,* which allowed one to see without being seen, seems to be a characteristic of the Ottoman era and reveals a certain opening of the house toward the outside world. The development of a resolutely vertical architecture, the series of reception rooms of greatly varied form and function *(taẖtabuš, mandara, maqʿad, qāʿa),* seem typical of a private architecture that was remarkably homogeneous.[22] But we know virtually nothing about the humbler types of houses, most of which have disappeared, or about the more majes-

34. Dār Bin ᶜAbdallah in Tunis (18th century)

35. Section of the Museum of Algiers (from Duthoit)

36. Courtyard of the house of Ǧamāl al-dīn al-Ḏahabī in Cairo (1637)

tic: the truly princely palaces were located in regions that were completely "renovated" during the nineteenth century, around Birka al-Fīl or Birka al-Azbakiyya.

3.2.3. Compared with this rather vertical and relatively compact architecture, the Syrian habitat seems to be characterized by its extension on the ground level and by the importance of its patios (which often take the shape of gardens with fountains, stone benches, and planted areas) with the typical element of the *īwān,* a rectangu-

37. *Maqᶜad* of Ǧabartī's house in Cairo (from P. Coste)

38. *Qāᶜa* of a house in Ḥūšqadam quarter in Cairo (from P. Coste)

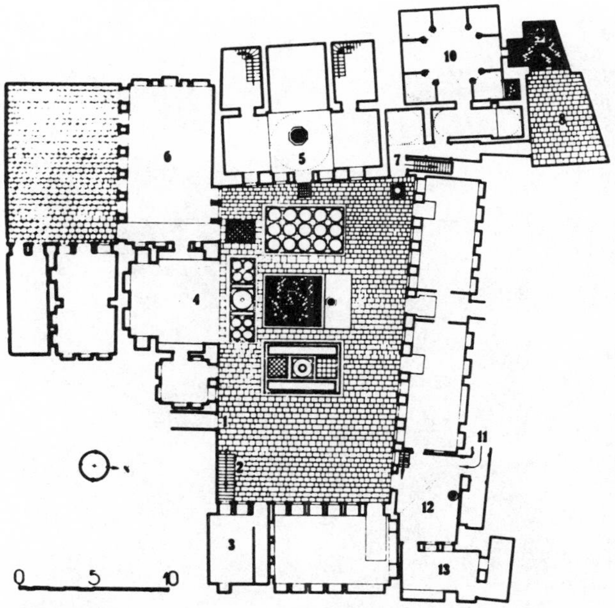

0 5 10

39. Plan of the Ġazzāla house in the Christian quarter of Aleppo (17th century) (from J. Sauvaget)

lar room opening on to the patio through an ogival arch. With its northward orientation and its utilization as a summer living room, the *īwān* is the equivalent of the Cairene *maqʿad,* but is on the ground floor. Cellars, used as storage rooms for food and as shelters from the heat of summer, are also typical of the houses of Aleppo. This naturally concerns important houses, sometimes veritable palaces. For Aleppo, the work of J. C. David makes it possible to measure the differences that existed between a rich habitat (inevitably exceptional) and a more common one. David distinguishes four types of traditional houses with a patio in the old town: the more modest (type I) have an average surface area of 83 square meters (including 34% for the patio); the larger (type III) measure anything up to 400 square meters (38% for the patio), and in some cases even 900 square meters (type IV).[23] The most important houses belonged to the merchant bourgeoisie of Aleppo. But even the smaller houses were inhabited by tradesmen and artisans, representative of the middle classes and not of the lower levels of the population. Research such as this, which should be extended to other cities, demonstrates that any work

40. Ağīqbāš house in Aleppo (18th century)

on the traditional habitat, when based solely on a study of the dwellings of the rich, is thoroughly inadequate.

3.3. "Atypical" Types of Individual Habitat

Researchers have recently taken an interest in types of individual habitat that do not correspond to "traditional" patterns. I shall present here some characteristic cases of "atypical" habitats of which future investigations will certainly provide more diverse examples.

3.3.1. Studying Cairo, Nelly Hanna has rightly drawn attention to the habitat of the social stratum situated between the bourgeoisie, who lived in the fine houses mentioned above, and the lower middle classes, who lived in the *rab*ᶜ (to which I shall return later on). This social stratum was numerically very important, since it included the majority of shopkeepers, artisans, and shaykhs. N. Hanna has undertaken a systematic study of the houses of this middle class. The house she first described (Bayt al-Isṭambulli)[24] gives a fairly accurate idea of these dwellings. It has no interior courtyard, for obvious reasons of economy (the wish to use all the available land to the fullest); if there is a courtyard, it is outside and is common to two contiguous houses. The house is divided into three to five living units located on several floors, with entrances grouped around staircases. These houses, which were evidently numerous in Cairo both in the central area and in the *ḥāra,* have characteristics that are in total contradiction to the generally admitted principles of the "Arab" house.

3.3.2. Just as significant from this point of view are the houses studied in Rosetta (Rašīd) by A. Lézine and A. Abdultawab.[25] These admirable houses are well known: Vivant Denon, as early as the eighteenth century, noticed that they resembled "our 14th century houses more than Oriental houses." Perhaps it is because of their "curious and unexpected appearance" (Herz) that they have been little studied and that researchers have hesitated to draw the conclusions they warranted as regards the "Arab" habitat. Outside, these houses present a refined decor based on the arrangement of windows with *mašrabiyya* and on the interplay of color and form made possible by the use of bricks. They can comprise four levels and they have no courtyard, at the utmost a shaft for light situated along a common wall. All the habitable rooms usually get both light and air from the streets (facing which there are two or three facades). It would naturally be tempting to dismiss the problem posed by these houses by describing them as pure and simple importations of Turkish models. But, if this Turkish influence is undeniable as regards details in construction and decor, it seems more probable that we are dealing here with an architecture of local tradition, an "architecture of the delta" concludes A. Lézine.

3.3.3. The question does not even arise for the Yemenite houses studied recently by Golvin and by Lewcock and Serjeant.[26] These have the following characteristics: exuberant decor on the facades, ornamental patterns of brick, accentuated by plaster wash, large open-

41. House in Rosetta

ings, projecting windows, claustra, stained glass; a vertical interior layout stretching over several floors, with rooms opening wide on to the exterior by a clever variety of protruding windows *(šubbāk* and *kušk)* and, naturally, an absence of any interior courtyard. There is such a total divergence from the traditional description of the "Arab" house that L. Golvin suggests making a parody of G. Marçais's definition, by stating that in the Yemen, "houses open wide onto the street, that the attractiveness and luxury of the facades are the objects sought by the architect and a sign of opulence for the master of the house." One could say the same for the houses of Jeddah, as

42. House in Ṣanʿā (from S. Ory)

recent research has shown both their "atypical" character and their striking similarities to the houses of Rosetta and Ṣanʿā.[27] The house with courtyard is more Mediterranean than Islamic, and it represents just one aspect (but the most common one) of a very varied typology on which much work remains to be done.

3.4. Collective Housing

Finally, one must attach more importance to collective housing than has been done up till now, and one must recognize the importance of the role it played in all the Arab cities. There were three main types of such housing: the "transitory" habitat (of the caravanserai type), the permanent habitat (of the *rabʿ* type), and the poorer habitat (of the *ḥawš* type).

3.4.1. We know that in nearly all the big Arab cities an important part of the population lived in caravanserais. They were, no doubt, mainly what one could describe as a more or less "unstabi-

43. House in Jeddah

lized" population. Merchants arriving from abroad or from the provinces and passing through the city settled in a caravanserai as they might in a hotel and had at their disposal both premises for their goods (normally laid out on the ground floor) and lodgings (usually a room on the second floor). We have already mentioned this fact when describing some of the types of caravanserai existing in big Arab cities.

There also lived in the caravanserais those military personnel not quartered in barracks; this is why, in Cairo, for example, during periods of crisis (when an expedition was being prepared), militia officers went around all the *wakāla* to gather their men together, and why, from time to time, soldiers were given orders to evacuate the *wakāla*. In Tunis many Turkish soldiers lodged likewise in *funduq*, in particular in the Suq al-ᶜAṭṭārin [T. J 6] and near the al-Qṣar Mosque [T. L 5].[28] The soldiers tended to bring not very commendable habits with them into the caravanserais, turning them into brothels and wine shops, a situation that often brought the authorities to take action and close (and sometimes even destroy) some of these places, apparently with no durable success. But one also found there a population composed of people coming from the provinces and installed in the capital for a more or less long period. Kabyles settling in Algiers in the caravanserais near Bāb ᶜAzzūn [AL. B 8] (the oil *funduq*) and natives of Djerba, Twātī, Wargliyya, and Zuwāwa, installed in the various *ukala* of Tunis, provide significant examples of this type of residence.[29] In Aleppo collective lodgings of the same kind were also known to exist: apart from the khan where merchants could rent a room and a store for their goods, there were *qaysāriyya* that were used as inns for poorer strangers, Arabs, and Bedouins.[30]

It is of course difficult to estimate what proportion of the population lodged in these collective residences. We do know that, in a town like Tunis, several thousand people lived in the *ukala*. D'Arvieux quotes the figure of 187 "caisseries" (compared with 68 khans) for Aleppo, at the end of the seventeenth century.[31] As there were in Cairo, under the Ottomans, about 360 *wakāla*, some of which could accommodate more than 100 residents, one can easily imagine the importance that the caravanserais played in lodging individuals. Indeed, though, on account of the often transitory character of their installation, residents of the caravanserais were less likely to appear in the successions of the *Maḥkama* registers, I have been able to identify 17 of them among the 334 individuals whose place of residence I have located in Cairo between 1776 and 1798, that is, 5%, a not inconsiderable proportion, the real proportion obviously being much greater. Out of this number, less than half are reported foreigners, which confirms that the *wakāla* were not used as lodgings solely by non-Egyptians. The average wealth of the caravanserai dwellers is characteristic of the middle class in Cairo: 53,128 paras compared with 109,101 paras, the general average (for 334 individuals).

3.4.2. Even more significant of the importance of this collective

44. *Rab*ᶜ of Tabbāna in Cairo

habitat is the Cairo *rab*ᶜ, which, as research stands at present, seems to be a purely Egyptian institution—an ancient one, however, since the existence of *rab*ᶜ is attested as early as the Mamluk period, and probably dates from even earlier.[32] Our information about the *rab*ᶜ is as complete as possible, since we have both very precise contemporary descriptions (especially in *waqf* documents) and still existing examples that can be studied with precision.[33] The *rab*ᶜ is a collective building used for rental that appears in two forms. In the isolated *rab*ᶜ, up to 15-odd apartments are distributed on two or three levels over a ground floor occupied by shop premises or warehouses. In the *rab*ᶜ*-wakāla,* up to 20 apartments occupy the two or three upper floors of the caravanserai, with which the *rab*ᶜ has no direct communication. In the two cases the general construction principles remain constant: the split-level apartments are arranged vertically (on two or three floors) with a double space allotted for the reception room *(riwāq);* they are accessible by common stairs or corridors; and they comprise a terrace on the upper level, the surface area by level averaging 30 square meters. The *rab*ᶜ, of which we have located 46, were generally situated near the main center of commercial activity, in the vicinity of the Qaṣaba (see Ill. 27). They were used as lodgings by a population of small artisans and shopkeepers: with an average wealth of 22,646 paras (1776–1798), these typical middle-class people would not have had the means of acquiring, or renting, a house near the center, but they could afford to rent or buy an apartment in a collective building. It is naturally difficult to estimate the percentage of the population who lived in the *rab*ᶜ*;* as many of the 360 Cairene *wakāla* included one *rab*ᶜ*;* their number must have well exceeded 100 or so, each being able to accommodate over 100 people. In fact, during perusal of the *Maḥkama* successions, I noted 29 inhabitants in *rab*ᶜ out of the total of 334 individuals studied, (nearly 10%), and if we consider only those individuals whose place of residence was in Qāhira (173), we note that there were 24 *rab*ᶜ inhabitants among them (13.9% of the total). Lodging in *rab*ᶜ was therefore a very common phenomenon in Cairo and could have involved 15,000 to 20,000 people.[34]

3.4.3. More widespread in the Arab world, but less well known, were the poorer collective dwellings called *ḥawš,* the existence of which is mentioned in Cairo and Aleppo. In Cairo the *ḥawš* were described by Jomard (in the *Description de l'Egypte)* as "great courtyards or enclosures full of four foot high shacks crammed with poor people living with their livestock."[35] We do not have any more precise information, but the location of 31 of these *ḥawš* by the *Description* enables us to understand their nature better: most of them were situated within the *ḥāra* zones, on the outskirts of Qāhira—exactly, therefore, in the regions occupied by the popular and poorer districts of Cairo.

What we know of the *ḥawš* in Syria is in exact accordance with the *Description.* The word does indeed designate a courtyard surrounded by very poor lodgings inhabited by different families. In

EL AHMAD

45. *Ḥawš* in the Qārliq quarter of Aleppo

Damascus, in the sixteenth century, a *ḥawš* situated in the Jewish quarter is described as follows in a *waqf* act: "The whole of the place *(al-makān)* near bāb Šarqī . . . which comprises a large open courtyard, around which, on all four sides, there are lodgings *(buyūt)*. . . . There are two wells for drinking water and eight lavatories in the courtyard . . . each lodging has a door giving onto the courtyard."[36] And it is obviously a *ḥawš* that the English traveler, A. Russell, describes under the name of "keisaria" in Aleppo, around 1750: "There is a kind of building, generally appropriated to the lower class of strangers, as Arabs, Kurds, other Turks of foreign extraction, and Armenian Christians. It is . . . a large area surrounded by a number of low, mean houses, each consisting of two or three rooms. The area is common to all the inhabitants and irregularly paved, except in front of the house door, where some bushes are planted. There is no fountain, but several draw wells. Of these keisarias a great number are scattered both in the town and suburbs."[37] We think, like A. Abdel Nour, that this layout, far from being a degradation of nobler forms, was perhaps an adaptation to the town of a rural type of habitat, which explains its location on the outskirts of cities and, in some cases, the presence of cattle. It corresponded to a certain conception of constructed space: "the poorer being unable to possess a private courtyard, organized constructed space so as to create a common courtyard, in urban buildings, probably in a spontaneous way."[38] There are no archaeological traces of these *ḥawš,* but we think that the street plan of the Qārliq district in northeast Aleppo is perhaps what remains of this type of poorer collective dwelling.

4. CONCLUSION

It would naturally be absurd to suggest replacing unsatisfactory stereotypes with just as questionable generalizations: the *predominance* of the house with a central courtyard in the Mediterranean Arab world is indisputable.

But, in the preceding remarks, I wished to call attention, on the one hand, to the limitations of the classical theory of the individual habitat: the occultation of regional, geographic, historical, and cultural factors (in the Mediterranean area) to the advantage of an exclusively religious issue tends to present the town as a geographical projection of a conception of the universe of which the modes of application to urban realities are never satisfactorily defined. On the other hand, I wished also to point out that one should not study merely exceptional types of houses, like palaces, but that a coherent study of habitat should be global, insofar as archaeological resources and historical sources allow. Such research, which at present is under way in Cairo, Damascus, and Aleppo, will, without doubt, show how varied the traditional Arab types of habitat really were, and how absurd it would be to suggest that such widely spread forms of collective and individual dwellings are just "atypical."[39]

Notes

1. See the books of Jacques Revault, *Palais et demeures de Tunis,* 4 vols. (Tunis, 1967–1978); and, for Cairo, the publications of the French research group: Alexandre Lézine, *Trois palais d'époque ottomane au Caire* (Cairo, 1972); Jacques Revault and Bernard Maury, *Palais et maisons du Caire* (Cairo), vol. I (1975), vol. II (1977), vol. III (1979) (with the collaboration of Mona Zakariya); Jean-Claude Garcin, Bernard Maury, Jacques Revault, and Mona Zakariya, *Palais et maisons du Caire, I, Epoque mameluke* (Paris, 1982); Bernard Maury, André Raymond, Jacques Revault, and Mona Zakariya, *Palais et maisons du Caire, II, Epoque ottomane* (Paris, 1983).

2. Alexandre Lézine, *Deux villes d'Ifriqiya* (Paris, 1971), 159–162. See the remarks of Antoine Abdel Nour on this point in *Introduction à l'histoire urbaine de la Syrie ottomane (XVIe–XVIIIe siècle),* (Beirut, 1982), 48–52.

3. Research in progress by Nelly Hanna: see her article, "Bayt al-Isṭambullī: An Introduction to the Cairene Middle Class House of the Ottoman Period," *Annales Islamologiques* 16 (1980).

4. André Raymond, *Artisans et commerçants au Caire au XVIIIème siècle,* 2 vols. (Damascus, 1974), II, 374: one *ẖuḍarī* (seller of vegetables), 145 paras in 1703; one coffee merchant, 8,849,660 paras in 1735. All these figures are expressed in Egyptian paras of constant value (see *Artisans,* I, liii–lv).

5. A. Abdel Nour, *Introduction,* 165.

6. Antoine Abdel Nour, "Types architecturaux et vocabulaire de l'habitat en Syrie," in Dominique Chevallier, ed., *L'Espace social de la ville arabe* (Paris, 1979), 82–83.

7. About the police of the suqs in Tunis see Etienne Buthaud, "Le gardiennage des souks de Tunis," *Revue de l'Institut des Belles Lettres Arabes, (IBLA)* 5 (1942).

8. Jacques Weulersse, "Antioche. Essai de géographie urbaine," *Bulletin d'Etudes Orientales (BEO)* 4 (1934).

9. I. W. J. Hopkins, "The Four Quarters of Jerusalem," *Palestine Exploration Quarterly* 103 (1971).

10. André Raymond, "Les quartiers de résidence des commerçants syriens et palestiniens au Caire," in the forthcoming *Mélanges Berque* (Paris, 1984).

11. J. Revault, *Palais,* II, 401.

12. G. Marty, "A Tunis: éléments allogènes et activités professionnelles," *IBLA* 11 (1948).

13. J. D. Latham, "Contribution à l'étude de l'émigration andalouse," and Slimane Mostafa Zbiss, "Présence espagnole à Tunis," in M. de Epalza and R. Petit, eds., *Etudes sur les Moriscos andalous en Tunisie* (Madrid, 1973). See also J. Revault, *Palais,* I, 43; II, 401; Robert Brunschvig, "Quelques remarques historiques sur les medersas de Tunisie," *Revue Tunisienne* 6 (1931), 281.

14. A. al-Ǧabartī, *ʿAǧāʾib al-āṯār,* 4 vols. (Būlāq, 1879), II. 3.

15. C. Niebuhr, *Voyage en Arabie,* 2 vols. (Amsterdam, 1776), I, 88.

16. André Raymond, "Essai de géographie des quartiers de résidence aristocratique au Caire au XVIIIème siècle," *Journal of Economic and Social History of the Orient (JESHO)* 6 (1963).

17. A. al-Ǧabartī, *ʿAǧāʾib,* IV, 40.

18. A. Raymond, "Essai de géographie des quartiers de résidence."

19. Jean-Claude David, "Alep, dégradation et tentatives actuelles de réadaptation," *BEO* 28 (1975). My map is deduced from David's figure 12.

20. In the *Encyclopédie de l'Islam,* 2d ed. (Leyde-Paris, 1965), II, 116, art. "dâr," Georges Marçais gives a description that is so classic that it deserves to be quoted at length: "The laying-out of a central empty space, surrounded by habitable rooms, does not, admittedly, belong exclusively to the Arab world. The same arrangement is characteristic of the primitive Roman house, with its atrium, and of the Hellenistic house, with its peristyle. . . . But this type of domestic architecture seems to offer Moslem life an ideal setting. It is naturally adapted to the patriarchal conception of the family. . . . It favours the secrecy with which the Moslem surrounds his private life. . . . The Moslem home, even when rich, presents a plain exterior, bare walls . . . and narrow and rare windows. . . . The main interest of this domestic architecture is the interior empty space. The courtyard is practically the main room of the house."

21. Georges Marçais, *L'Architecture musulmane d'Occident* (Paris, 1954), 437–445, 474–481, and "La maison Nord-Africaine," *Cahiers des Arts et Techniques d'Afrique du Nord* 7 (1974); and, for Tunis, J. Revault, *Palais.*

22. See the various publications of A. Lézine, J. Revault, B. Maury, M. Zakariya, J.-C. Garcin, and A. Raymond, already mentioned (note 1). More especially see Jacques Revault, "L'Architecture domestique au Caire à l'époque ottomane," in Bernard Maury et al., *Palais et maisons du Caire, II, Epoque ottomane.*

23. Jean-Claude David, "Les paysages urbains d'Alep," thesis, University of Lyon II, 1972, and "Alep, dégradation," 20–32, pl. 12. This typology was first defined for Tunis by G. Cladel and P. Revault in *Medina, approche typologique* (Tunis, 1970).

24. N. Hanna, "Bayt al-Isṭambullī."

25. Alexandre Lézine and A. R. Abdultawab, "Introduction à l'étude des maisons anciennes de Rosette," *Annales Islamologiques* 10 (1972).

26. Lucien Golvin, "Quelques aspects de l'architecture domestique en République Arabe du Yémen," in P. Bonnenfant, ed., *La Péninsule Arabique d'aujourd'hui* (Paris, 1982); R. Lewcock and R. D. Serjeant, "The Houses of Ṣanʿāʾ" in *Ṣanʿāʾ* (London, 1983).

27. See Talal M. Kamel Kurdi, "Influence of Arabian Tradition on the Old City of Jeddah," in Ismail Serageldin and Samir El-Sadek, eds., *The Arab City. Its Character and Islamic Cultural Heritage* (N.p., 1982).

28. See, in Cairo, the events of 1105/1694 ("Kitāb al-Tarāǧim," ms. Cairo, DK t. 2269, 860; "Zubda," ms. London, B. M. add. 9972, 26a); and, in Tunis, the incidents of 1743 (Ḥammūda b. ^{c}Abd al-^{c}Azīz, "al-Kitāb al-Bāšī," ms. Tunis B.N., Or. 351, p. 462).

29. Claude Antoine Rozet, *Voyage dans la Régence d'Alger,* 3 vols. (Paris, 1833), II, 16, 67; René Lespès, *Alger* (Paris, 1930), 181, 182; Pierre Boyer, *La vie quotidienne à Alger à la veille de l'intervention française* (Paris, 1963), 164; and, for Tunis, G. Marty, "A Tunis: éléments allogènes," 165–170, and "Les Algériens à Tunis," *IBLA* 11 (1948), 309–326.

30. J. Sauvaget, *Alep,* 222.

31. L. d'Arvieux, *Mémoires,* 6 vols. (Paris, 1735), VI, 434, 437.

32. Laila ^{c}Ali Ibrahim, "Middle Class Living Units in Mamluk Cairo," *Art and Archaeology Research Papers (AARP)* (1978).

33. On the *rab^{c}* see M. de Chabrol, "Essai sur les moeurs des habitants modernes de l'Egypte," in *Description de l'Egypte,* Etat Moderne, vol. II-2 (Paris, 1822), 516–517; Edward W. Lane, *Manners and Customs of the Modern Egyptians,* rev. ed. (London, 1954), 21; Marcel Clerget, *Le Caire,* 2 vols. (Cairo, 1934), I, 316–317; Mona Zakariya, "Le *rab^{c}* de Tabbāna," *Annales Islamologiques* 16 (1980); André Raymond, "The *rab^{c}*: A Type of Collective Housing," publication no. 4 of *The Aga Khan Award for Architecture* (1980).

34. In her study of the *ḥāra* of Sukkariyya, "The Concept of the Ḥāra," *Annales Islamologiques* 15 (1979), Nawāl al-Messiri Nadim remarks that the 25 flats of the *rab^{c}* could accommodate 35 families (171 individuals) out of 117 families (639 individuals) for the whole *ḥāra.*

35. E. F. Jomard, "Ville du Caire," in *Description de l'Egypte,* Etat Moderne, vol. II-2 (Paris, 1822), 662, 696. See R. Dozy, *Supplément aux dictionnaires arabes,* 2 vols. (Leide-Paris, 1927), I, 336.

36. A. Abdel Nour, *Introduction,* 132.

37. A. Russell, *The Natural History of Aleppo,* 2 vols. (London, 1794), I, 36.

38. A. Abdel Nour, *Introduction,* 133–134.

39. See the significant remarks of Clerget on the *rab^{c}* after a precise description of its structure and a correct appraisal of its importance in Cairo: "Le rab est une dérogation aux coutumes de l'Islam et à l'adaptation au milieu physique" *(Le Caire,* I, 317).

CHAPTER FOUR

Imperial Art, Local Tradition, and Innovation

1. INTRODUCTION

I have already pointed out that the Ottoman era in Arab countries has not only been globally underestimated but has even been subject to derogatory assessments. Considered as an era of foreign rule (sometimes termed "colonial"), it has mainly been judged negatively, and therefore has been nearly totally left in the shadows.[1] The most severely judged deficiencies are those which concern the intellectual and artistic domains: "The literature, the sciences and the arts, which had shone so brilliantly in the past, grew dull in 16th, 17th and 18th century Cairo: there is less original thought, little is written, few buildings are constructed, and if repairs are sometimes carried out, most frequently ruins are left to accumulate. . . . Egypt seems plunged into a deep sleep" writes Marcel Colombe, a good "connoisseur" of the Ottoman period.[2] Even E. Pauty, who has done so much toward the rediscovery of this period, seems obliged to apologize for his interest in Egyptian monuments of the Ottoman period: "One must admit that a sort of disrepute attends this art, considered as not being very local and as being of questionable aesthetic attractiveness."[3]

There are objective reasons for the discredit in which the architectural activities of the Ottoman era have been held. But it is also largely explainable by the very limited knowledge we have of this period. Relatively recent, the Ottoman monuments have been slighted in classification policies followed, with varying degrees of success, in the different Arab countries, ever since the end of the last century. Many have disappeared. Those that remain have been studied very little. Published works have been equally scarce; and, in many cases, the most elementary architectural information is wanting. Turkish art specialists have concerned themselves only in a marginal way with these remains of an inevitably uninnovative provincial art, which explains some surprising inaccuracies.[4] Specialists in the art and architecture of the Arab countries concerned have considered this period as being neither representative nor original; they have taken little interest in it and have often hastily tended to call "Ottoman" structures that in reality owe little to the influence of the capital and its "Turkish" art.

Our information varies greatly, depending on the regions concerned; here again, Egypt is the country we are least ill-informed about. After the pioneer works of Pauty and of Hautecoeur and Wiet,[5] two studies have recently revived interest in monuments of the Ottoman era in Cairo, that of J. A. Williams (1969) and that of M. Rogers (1978).[6] One must hope that this recent development will continue and spread to other regions of the Arab world. Renewed interest is particularly urgent in the case of Ottoman monuments insofar as a great number are nonreligious buildings (caravanserais, private houses, fountains, public baths), which are thus the most threatened by the very rapid deterioration of the monumental patrimony that is observable at present in most Arab towns.

The Ottoman period has played, in fact, a great part in the constitution of urban decor in Arab cities: it has left us a considerable number of monuments; from a quantitative point of view, it is sufficient to point out that even in Cairo, a city where these constructions have not aroused great interest on the part of the authorities, classified monuments of the Ottoman era number 199, a figure comparable to that of the Mamluk monuments (233) for a scarcely longer period of time (281 years as against 257). Generally speaking, the "traditional" Arab cities we know are a legacy of the Ottoman period that lasted, depending on the case, three or four centuries and that inevitably left a strong impression on urban structures. Finally, a close study of this architecture, making allowance for exterior influences and local traditions, would enable one to draw significant conclusions concerning the very character of Ottoman rule and about the way it affected the cultural and artistic activities of the countries over which it held sway.[7]

2. "IMPERIAL" ART

The phenomenon that is immediately striking, when one considers a production of such considerable numerical importance (nearly 200 classified edifices in Cairo, more than 100 monuments preserved in Aleppo, 50 or so in Baghdad),[8] is that the actual number of what one could call monuments of "Ottoman" style is really quite limited. We have located a total of 15 important monuments of the "mosque" type that can be related to the models presented by the capital of the empire.

2.1. Chronological Classification

A chronological classification of these monuments is very significant:

• The Mosque of Sulaymān Pasha, built by this governor in the Cairo Citadel, in 1528, is a monument of pure Ottoman tradition (apparent in its courtyard, T-shaped prayer hall, minaret) that Goodwin connects with the plan of the Mosque of Firuz Bey in Milas (dated 1394). But the decoration (especially that of the *miḥrāb*) is unquestionably Egyptian [C. S 2].[9]

• The Ḫusrawiyya Mosque, the most ancient "Ottoman" monument constructed in Aleppo, was built for Ḫusrū Pasha in 1544 by the great architect Sinan, then at the beginning of his career: the portico, which comprises five domes, extends beyond the prayer hall, as in the Manisa Mosque (1522), an arrangement that later would often be repeated (e.g., by Sinan himself in the Mosque of Ibrāhīm

Pasha in Istanbul in 1551). Some awkwardness in its realization perhaps reveals a lack of experience on the part of the builder [A. Q 16].[10]

• The ʿĀdiliyya Mosque, built, in Aleppo again, by Muḥammad Pasha (1555), belongs to a type closely related to the Ḫusrawiyya, but with a double portico, a fairly original device that had been used a short time before by Sinan in the construction of the Mihrimah Mosque of Usküdar (approximately 1548) [A. Q 14].[11]

• The *takiyya* (convent) and the *madrasa* built on the orders of Sultan Sulaymān in Damascus, between 1554 and 1566, are two typically "Ottoman" monuments in which Sinan evoked the great edifices of Istanbul, on a reduced scale. On this royal foundation, intended for the use of pilgrims, local traditions reappear only in details of the decoration.[12]

• The Mosque of Sinān Pasha in Būlāq (1571) is a building based on an "Ottoman" plan, comprising a large portico developed on three sides; its facade, however, is profoundly influenced by the great Mamluk traditions. This monument, one of the most successful of Ottoman Cairo, would later be purely and simply duplicated by Muḥammad Bey.[13]

• The two nearly contemporaneous Mosques of Murād and of Darwīš Pasha, built just outside the walls of Damascus (1572 and 1574, respectively), also combine an "Ottoman" plan (with domes) with facades of typical Syrian style: the minaret of the Murādiyya is of Mamluk inspiration, whereas that of the Darwīšiyya is Ottoman [D. C 4 and D 8].[14]

• The Bahrāmiyya Mosque of Aleppo, constructed by Bahrām Pasha about 1583, evokes the Mosque of ʿAlī Pasha in Tokat (1573), but with a dome whose size was reduced because of construction difficulties; and a vast apse reminiscent of certain most ancient Turkish monuments (also to be found in the Mosque of Mehmed Agha, 1585) [A. P 11].[15]

• The Mosque of Sinān Pasha in Damascus (1590) also seems to belong to a type of which the Mosque of Tokat is a good example (1573), but its minaret, covered with green tiles, is quite original. The facade, like that of the mosques of 1572 and 1574, is treated in a strongly Mamluk architectural and decorative manner [D. D 5].[16]

• Built in Cairo in 1610 by ʿUṯmān Agha Dār al-Saʿāda, and afterward attributed to his mistress, the sultana Ṣafiya, wife of Murād III and mother of Muḥammad III, the Mosque of Malika Ṣafiya

46. Ḫusrawiyya Mosque in Aleppo

47. Takiyya of Sultan Sulaymān in Damascus

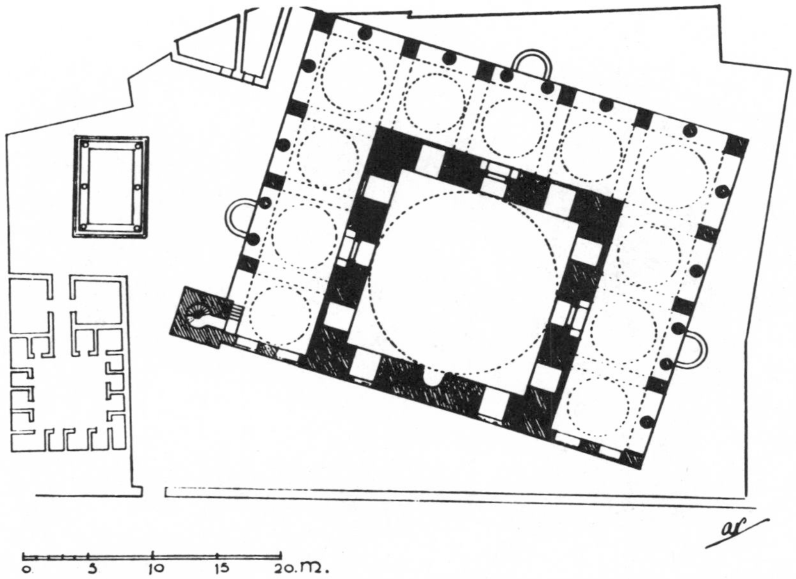
0 5 10 15 20.m.

48. Plan of the Sinān Pasha Mosque in Būlāq (from Patricolo)

49. Sinān Pasha Mosque in Būlāq

50. Darwīš Pasha Mosque in Damascus

is the most royal and the most purely "Ottoman" of all the Cairo mosques. Its plan reproduces that of many important religious buildings of Istanbul (particularly the Mosque of Djerrah Pasha, 1594) and of Edirne (Selimiye, 1575), but on a notably smaller scale, with a square courtyard inside a portico covered with small domes, preceding the square-shaped prayer hall. The high semicircular perrons that give access to the courtyard and contribute to the originality of the monument remind one by their size of the rectangular steps of Yeni Valide in Istanbul (before 1605), the general plan of which, moreover, is comparable [C. O 8].[17]

• Built in 1660 on the initiative of the *odjaq* (militia) of Algiers, to serve the Hanafite cult, the al-Ǧadīd Mosque (or Mosque "of the Fishery") has, owing to its central dome and its four corner domes, an "Ottoman" air that is hardly, however, confirmed by its plan: Marçais likens it to the Kilisse Ǧāmi^{c}; Dokali speaks of a "paleo-Christian" plan and evokes the Ulu Cami of Bursa. Its square minaret has a definitely Maghribian look [AL. F 8].[18]

• There is no question, however, as to the origins of the plan of

51. Sinān Pasha Mosque in Damascus

the Mosque of Sidi Mehrez, built in Tunis by Muḥammad Bey in 1696. The arrangement of the domes above the prayer hall (a central dome set on four half domes and four smaller corner domes) is that of the Sultan Aḥmad Mosque in Istanbul (1617); and it would be, in fact, totally "Ottoman" in character if it had a minaret in keeping with its style and if the enveloping portico were not so obviously "Tunisian" [T. B 4].[19]

• The ʿUṯmāniyya Madrasa, built in Aleppo in 1730 by ʿUṯmān Pasha al-Dūrakī, is a monument of an Ottoman style as pronounced as that of the Takiyya and the Madrasa of Sulaymān built in Damascus nearly two centuries earlier. The minaret, in particular, is a perfect Syrian example of a model widely used during the Ottoman

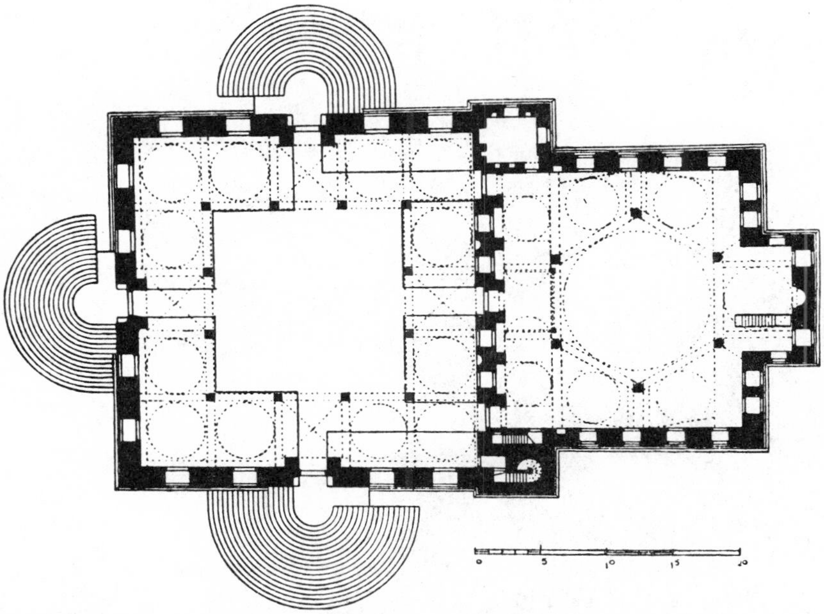

52. Mosque of Malika Ṣafiya in Cairo (from Patricolo)

53. Mosque of Malika Ṣafiya

54. Al-Ǧadīd Mosque in Algiers

55. Mosque of Sidi Mehrez in Tunis

era. Nevertheless, the presence of two *īwān* on either side of the triple-domed portico gives the monument a local touch, especially since the large courtyard, surrounded by 42 lodgings, evokes the courtyards of Syrian houses with its rectangular basin and its plantations [A. J 17].[20]

• The Qaymariyya Mosque, built in 1743 in Damascus by Fatḥī Efendi, a *daftardār* (treasurer) who belonged to a family of notables, is a perfect example of a monument with a plan of obviously "Ottoman" origin (a portico with three small domes giving access to a prayer hall covered by a large dome) but with a decor so profoundly influenced by Syro-Mamluk traditions (stone of alternate white, black, and ochre colors) that the imported character of the architecture is somewhat overshadowed by the local exuberance of the patterns of color [D. H 3].[21]

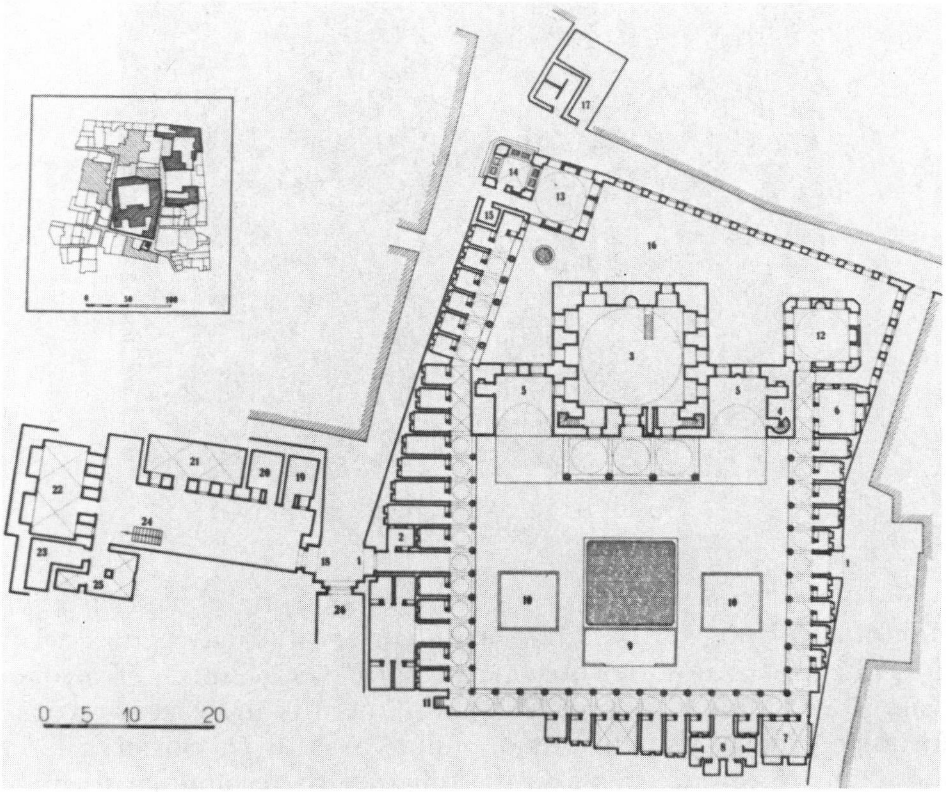

56. ʿUṯmāniyya Madrasa in Aleppo (plan by Kh. Moaz in J. Sauvaget)

57. Qaymariyya Mosque in Damascus

• In 1774, on the eve of the collapse of Mamluk rule in Egypt, Muḥammad Bey Abū Ḏahab, who ruled Egypt briefly between 1772 and 1775, had a mosque constructed in the very center of Cairo, opposite the Mosque al-Azhar. This monument is an exact copy of the Mosque of Sinān Pasha in Būlāq, built two centuries earlier, the only noteworthy difference being in the minaret. Its rectangular form and its four levels recall, with such precision, the nearby minaret of the Madrasa al-Ġūrī, that one can only imagine that the architect (or the

58. Mosque of Muḥammad Bey Abū Ḏahab in Cairo

patron) deliberately wanted to evoke, in a typically "Ottoman" monument, the characteristics of Mamluk national art [C. K 5].[22]

2.2. Character

It is true that out of the important number of monuments of the sixteenth to eighteenth centuries that have disappeared some were "Ottoman." In Algiers, French occupation resulted in the complete destruction or the irremediable mutilation of several important mosques built during this period. Elsewhere, neglect or modernization are responsible for many losses. In Cairo, for instance, we know that the minaret of the Iskandar Pasha Mosque (built in 1555) was a monument of pure "Ottoman" style, but the mosque was totally destroyed at the end of the nineteenth century.[23] Nevertheless, from what we know we can assume that the "Ottoman" production represents only a very slight part of the hundreds of religious monuments built from the sixteenth to the eighteenth century in the Arab provinces.

This phenomenon should not surprise us. Although the Turkish ethnic group played an eminent role in the Ottoman Empire, the imperial government left a fairly high degree of autonomy to the subject communities; and, on the cultural level in particular, no serious attempt at imposing Turkish ways seems to have been made in the Arab-populated regions. The respect the Turks had for the Arabs' language and culture, which were so closely connected with the Muslim religion, explains this absence of any "cultural colonialism," with sometimes surprising consequences: although the members of the ruling institution were mainly Turkish or spoke the Turkish language, and although the more important judicial dignitaries were recruited in Istanbul, the succession registers of the *Qisma ʿAskariyya* (military section) of the Tribunal of Cairo were written nearly entirely in Arabic as early as the sixteenth century. Rare indeed are the Arab countries where inscriptions in the Turkish language represent a significant part of the monumental epigraphy. Far from thinking of imposing Turkish culture and traditions in Egypt, Sultan Salīm apparently contemplated building or decorating in the Mamluk style in Istanbul and, in order to do so, had a certain number of Egyptian craftsmen transferred to the capital as well as some decorative elements taken from Cairo monuments.[24] The influence exerted by the art of the capital in Arab provinces therefore had an intermittent character, and it is obvious that there was no systematic policy in this regard.

As much as their relatively limited number, the chronological spacing and the geographical distribution of architectural creations in "Ottoman" style appear to be significant. Of 15 monuments mentioned earlier, 9 date from the sixteenth century and only 3 each from the seventeenth and eighteenth centuries, which seems to correspond to the contrast between a period during which the imperial government, and its local representatives, may have wanted to assert Ottoman power, then in full expansion, and a period of decline of the empire. As for their location, one contrasts the predominance of

Syria (Aleppo, 4; Damascus, 5) and of Egypt (Cairo, 4) with the weak position of the Maghrib (Tunis and Algiers, 1). The number of "Ottoman" constructions is obviously linked to a proximity to the center of power and, no doubt, to the vigor of the Ottoman presence. The faraway Maghrib was little affected by a building movement that was very marked in Syria. The total absence of Iraq is cause for surprise: one would have thought that in this territory, where the Persians fought for so long with the Ottomans, Istanbul and its representatives would have wanted to express their final victory and their authority with buildings of prestige in the "official" style. Nothing of the sort happened, and the main reason one can suggest for this is the strength of local traditions and patronage,[25] but one must also recognize the fact that Ottoman rule in Iraq was definitely consolidated only during the seventeenth century (after a period of Iranian reoccupation of Baghdad), at a time when the most active phase of building in "Ottoman" style was nearly over.

2.3. Political Motivations

The foregoing remarks seem to demonstrate the prevailing political character of these constructions in a style that one can call "imperial" It is therefore quite natural to notice that nearly all these great religious edifices, the very style of which was a reminder of the Ottoman presence, were the work of representatives of the Porte (9 out of 15) and sometimes even of the sultan and his entourage (2 monuments). This seems self-evident for the three great mosques built in Aleppo in the sixteenth century; they are, so to speak, material representations of Ottoman sovereignty. In the most central part of the town, within the Madīna, the urban landscape of the great town of northern Syria is marked by the soaring minarets and domes of Turkish style.

One must similarly consider the great "imperial" structures erected in Damascus in a zone situated outside the walls, to the west of the town, during the second half of the sixteenth century (1554–1590). The Takiyya and the Madrasa of Sulaymān showed, in a most spectacular way, the sultan's interest in the pilgrimage, of which Damascus, along with Cairo, was a rallying point. The three great Mosques of Murād, Darwīš, and Sinān, three successive pashas, concretized, at the very entrance to Damascus, the power of the Ottomans. The Mosque of Sulaymān Pasha, built in 1528 in the Citadel of Cairo, on a site overlooking the city, opposite the Madrasa of Sultan Ḥasan (which, in a way, symbolized the defeated Mamluk rule), no doubt had the same demonstrative value. That of Sinān Pasha in Būlāq (the main port of Cairo, particularly as regards relations with the Mediterranean, that is, with Turkey and the countries of the empire) was the first visible sign of the Ottoman presence upon arrival in Cairo. The Malika Ṣafiya Mosque, built near Bāb Zuwayla, carried the same message on the south road.

Evident in the case of monuments erected in the sixteenth century, at a time when Ottoman authority was being established and asserted through constructions by the imperial government and its representatives, political intent also seems to be present in later creations, which one can often interpret as manifestations of allegiance by nearly autonomous local authorities. The al-Ǧadīd Mosque of Algiers was built in 1660 on the orders of the *odjaq* for the use of the Hanafites shortly after the revolution of 1659, which had enabled the militia to deprive the pasha of all his powers. The building of a monument of "imperial" style could be considered as a sort of monumental reaffirmation of Ottoman sovereignty in Algiers. In Tunis the Sidi Mehrez Mosque was built by Muḥammad Bey whom the *odjaq* of Algiers had just restored to the throne (1686) and whose authority over the Regency was confirmed by the sultan in 1691. The monument, of marked Ottoman appearance, built between 1692 and 1696, constituted a kind of recognition of vassalage, all the more opportune as the mounting difficulties with the *odjaq* of Algiers, which were to result in another expedition against Tunis in 1694, incited the Muradite sovereign to ensure the support, or at least the neutrality, of the imperial government.

One can interpret the construction by Muḥammad Bey Abū Ḏahab, in 1774, of the pastiche of the Būlāq Mosque of Sinān Pasha in the same way. The Egyptian emir had just succeeded ʿAlī Bey, whose attempt to openly free himself from Ottoman supervision he had helped to quell; though he himself probably sought total control over Egypt, he was prepared to accept the outward appearance of submission to the Sublime Porte. The construction of a mosque of "Ottoman" style on a prestigious site was tantamount to visibly reasserting his loyalty toward the sultan and confirming other, similar decisions: a return to a currency coined in the sultan's name; a promise to resume sending the tribute; and a respectful reception of the new pasha, installed in 1773 after a long vacancy.[26] The style of the mosque therefore had a significance which was meant to be understood both by the representatives of the Ottoman government and by the Egyptian population.

2.4. *Dimensions of the Buildings*

The size of these monuments of "Ottoman" style justifies some remarks. They are edifices of modest dimensions if compared with the imposing architectural complexes built in Istanbul during the same period. The first (and main) explanation lies in the limited means available to simple governors who were generally more concerned about deriving as much profit as they could from their functions than about leaving a monumental memorial at the end of their usually brief stay. This accounts for an obvious reduction in scale in comparison with the sultan's constructions, and also with the more impressive monuments that the sovereigns of previous dynasties had raised to their own glory (e.g., those of the Mamluks of Cairo). Although generally moderate, the levying of tributes *(ḫazīna)* for the Imperial Treasury had the same effect. Michael Rogers gives the concern for economy as the main reason for the success that the public fountain *(sabīl)* had in Cairo during the Ottoman era, since building this type of monument of modest dimensions made it possible to realize a pious work and to leave a lasting mark in the urban landscape at relatively little cost.[27]

It is equally possible that technical reasons account for both the small number of monuments and their size. Economic development had so increased the congestion in the urban centers that there was hardly any room left for new creations of great size. This factor was to work particularly against the building of religious edifices in the "Ottoman" style, which could not develop properly except on fairly vast sites of regular shape. On the contrary, a long architectural tradition had taught Egyptian builders, for instance, how to fit monuments in the Mamluk style into overcrowded urban areas, which may explain why this type of construction remained so popular in Cairo during the sixteenth to eighteenth centuries.[28] It is thus understandable that, except in Aleppo, where there were reserves of land in the southern part of the Madīna, most "Ottoman" monuments were constructed outside urban centers.

2.5. Originality

One cannot expect these provincial monuments to display great architectural originality and even less to show an innovative character. They generally belonged to types that had already been experimented with elsewhere, usually in Istanbul or in the main provincial cities of Anatolia, and they were in keeping with a tradition the essential characteristics of which were already firmly fixed. However, they are generally not mere copies of monuments built in other towns; moreover, original creators seem to have intervened in a certain number of cases, such as the famous Sinan (in the Ḫusrawiyya Mosque of Aleppo and in the Takiyya and Madrasa of Sulaymān in Damascus).

On the other hand, one is struck by the builders' tendency to incorporate into such typical monuments details attesting the vitality of local traditions and also the ability of the native architects and craftsmen to fit them into a different architectural context. In most of the edifices we have mentioned, these traditions appear in more or less discreet touches: the Syrian *īwān* of the ʿUtmāniyya Madrasa of Aleppo, the enveloping portico of the Mehrez Mosque in Tunis, the minarets in local tradition of the al-Ǧadīd Mosque in Algiers or of the Mosque of Muḥammad Bey in Cairo, the facades entirely treated in "national" style of the mosques of Damascus and of that of Sinān Pasha in Būlāq. The most "official" art thus made allowance for regional styles, the persistence of which, during four centuries of Ottoman rule, is a very impressive phenomenon.

3. THE PERMANENCE OF LOCAL ARTISTIC TRADITION

Already appreciable in constructions built in "official" style, the permanence of native traditions appears above all in monuments of "local" style that make up the greater part of the architectural production in the Arab provinces of the empire. The numerical preponderance of monuments where these national traditions are expressed is evident in the very regions where the "imperial" style knew its greatest diffusion. In Aleppo, "Ottoman" edifices represent only a small proportion of the mosques built between the sixteenth and the eighteenth centuries (of which we have identified 30 or so). In Cairo the 4 mosques mentioned above are to be compared with the total of 34 mosques built between 1517 and 1798 that are classified today. This predominance is even more overwhelming in the provinces farther away from the center.

3.1. The Case of Iraq

This is, in particular, the case of Iraq where the traces left by official architecture are imperceptible and where, for more than two centuries, religious art developed according to local traditions. These traditions are, moreover, so different in Mosul and in Baghdad that we can qualify them as "Upper Mesopotamian" and "Iranian." In Mosul architectural production depended largely on private patronage, even during the time of the Ǧalīlī. This rather exceptional situation may account for the persistence of a religious architecture, the most marked characteristic of which is the use of brick in minarets for decorative purposes, in conformity with a very ancient tradition, apparent in the example of the great "Nūriyya" Mosque (1170). On a more modest scale, this type of decoration reappears during the whole Ottoman period: in the al-ᶜUmariyya (1563) [M. W 16], Ḫazām (before 1577), and Šahrsūq (1682) mosques, the brick motifs are enhanced by a background of turquoise ceramic. This tradition was continued during the eighteenth century, with a tendency to a certain monotony in its realization, as can be seen in the al-Aġawāt Mosque (1702) [M. M 20] and finally in the Mosque of Bāb al-Bayḍ (1779).

Nothing could be more different from this art of Upper Mesopotamia than the architecture that remained in favor in Baghdad for two centuries, an architecture where the use of earthenware tiles for decorating domes and minarets calls to mind Persian influence, although the builders were virtually always Ottoman pashas. The permanence and originality of this decoration are striking from the end of the sixteenth century to the beginning of the nineteenth cen-

59. Al-ᶜUmariyya Mosque in Mosul

tury. One can mention as examples: the Mosques al-Murādiyya (1570), al-Wazīr (1599), al-Ḫāṣikī (1658) [B. K 24], Ḥasan Pasha (1704), ᶜAlī Efendi (1711), al-ᶜĀdiliyya (1754), al-Nuᶜmāniyya (1771), al-Aḥmadiyya (1796), and finally the Ḥaydarḫāna Mosque (1826) [B. N 17]. In the general structure, the use of ceramics, the presence of epigraphic decor, the continuity is impressive; whatever the nature of the government (Ottoman pashas or Mamluk governors), and despite constantly strained political relations with Persia, Baghdad appears as still belonging to the domain of Iranian architecture.

60. Al-Aġawāt Mosque in Mosul

3.2. Mamluk Tradition in Cairo

If I elaborate further on the preservation of the local traditions in Cairene architecture, it is naturally because of the originality of an art so deeply implanted during the Mamluk era that it even imposed itself on the Ottoman conquerors; but it is also because the

61. Al-Ḫāṣikī Mosque in Baghdad

progress of research in Cairo makes it possible to come to more precise conclusions for this city than for anywhere else.

For three centuries, religious art continued to develop there in accordance with the architectural tradition that had filled the city with magnificent monuments. Apart from a few exceptions, the ruling pashas and emirs built monuments in a style that can rightly be called "neo-Mamluk."[29] Mamluk plans continued to be used until the very end of the eighteenth century, and the decoration remained pre-

62. Ḥaydarḫāna Mosque in Baghdad

dominantly Mamluk, no doubt partly because Cairo craftsmen were accustomed to handling these techniques and materials, but also certainly because this art was considered as wholly national and was appreciated as such.[30]

I shall limit myself to a few significant examples of this predilection and this remarkable loyalty to Mamluk architecture.

• Built in 1568 by Maḥmūd Pasha, between the Cairo Citadel and the Madrasa of Sultan Ḥasan, the Maḥmūdiyya Mosque is com-

63. Maḥmūdiyya Mosque in Cairo

pletely Mamluk in its plan (which evokes that of the great adjoining *madrasa,* 1356) and in all the details of its decoration (where the influence of the nearby Mosque of Qanbāy al-Sayfī Amīr Aḫūr, 1503, is also visible), except in regard to the minaret [C. S 5].[31]

• The al-Burdaynī Mosque, built from 1616 to 1629, is in striking contrast with the nearby, and nearly contemporaneous, Mosque of Malika Ṣafiya (1610), which is, as we have seen, one of the most

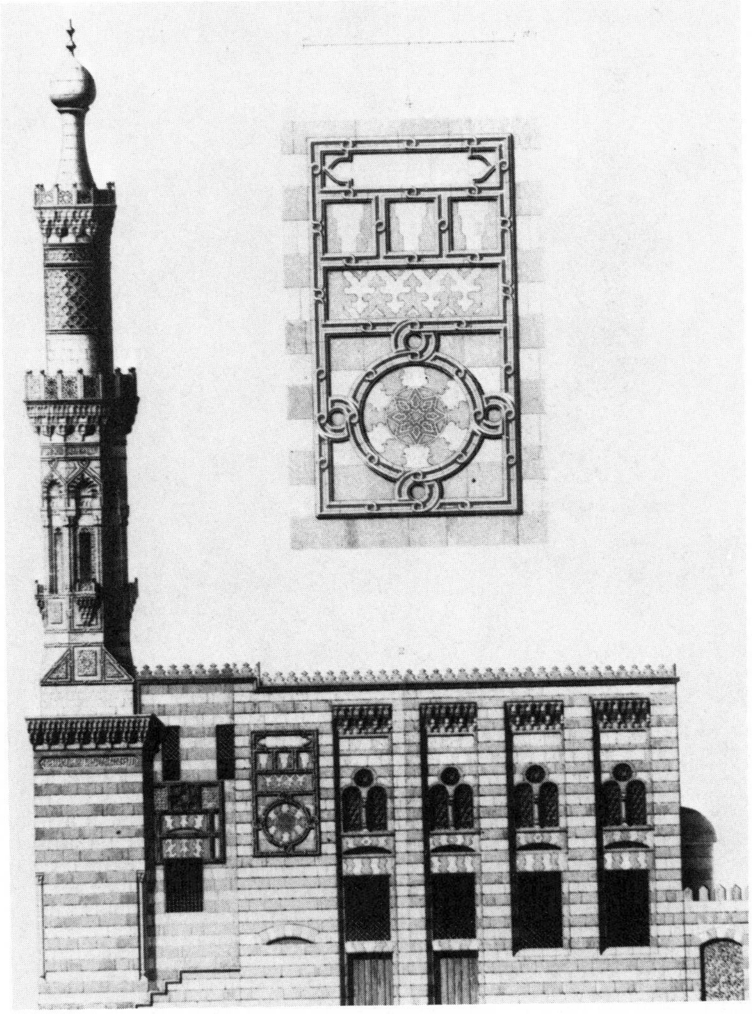

64. Al-Burdaynī Mosque in Cairo (from E. Prisse d'Avennes)

typical "Ottoman" monuments to be found in the Arab provinces. This mosque of the seventeenth century, "Saracenic in all its details," as Briggs writes, shows, in a most striking way, the strength of Mamluk tradition in Cairo. It is a monument that could easily be dated from the time of Qāytbāy if it were not for a certain degeneration of the decoration (especially noticeable in the *miḥrāb*). The minaret is a perfectly successful pastiche of the monuments of the

65. ʿUṯmān Katẖudā Mosque in Cairo

Burjite (Circassian) era, both in its structure as a whole and in its details: three levels, successively square, polygonal, and circular; balconies supported by *muqarnas* (stalactites)[C. O 7].[32]

• The mosque built in 1734, near the Birka Azbakiyya, by ʿUṯmān Katẖudā Qāzdaġlī, the leader of the Janissaries and the chief emir in Cairo between 1730 and 1736, belongs to the Mamluk type, with an open courtyard and a traditional prayer hall comprising three rows of columns parallel to the *qibla* wall. The rather austere facade

66. Yūsuf Čurbağī (al-Hayātim) Mosque in Cairo

again takes up Mamluk themes. The typically Ottoman minaret, alone, and a few decorative elements (ceramics and a wooden coffered ceiling with beams) make it truly possible to give this monument its real date [C. K 13].[33] ʿUṯmān's heir, ʿAbdarraḥmān Katẖudā (died 1776), one of the greatest builders ever known in Cairo, was usually inspired by this same national vein in his numerous constructions.[34]

• The Mosque of Yūsuf Čurbağī (al-Hayātim) (1763) is a monument that resumes the tradition of the cruciform plan: Hautecoeur describes it as a "contracted madrasa" and evokes, in this case, the cemetery of the caliphs. The composition of its facade and portal is Mamluk, but with a wealth of decoration that indicates an appreciable evolution in comparison with the models followed [C. R 11].[35]

Mamluk inspiration did not cease until the end of the eighteenth century, and was followed with such scrupulous fidelity that it is sometimes very difficult to decide whether we see a reconstruction or a simple restoration of a previously built monument. The Mosque of Maḥmūd Muḥarram is a typical example of this confusion of styles: its Mamluk appearance is no proof that the great merchant did not totally rebuild it in 1792, following a traditional model [C. G 5].[36]

The permanence of Mamluk influence is particularly striking in Cairo in the case of the *sabīl* (public fountains), which are the most frequent type of construction of the Ottoman era.[37] One of the oldest examples of these *sabīl,* built by a governor of Cairo in 1535, the Ḫusrū Pasha Fountain, is a pastiche on a slightly reduced scale of the al-Ġūrī Sabīl, built only a few years earlier (1503–1504) and situated nearby. The imitation is obvious in both the decoration and the epigraphy, but the Ḫusrū Pasha Sabīl is nevertheless a very fine monument, admirably located and rightly admired [C. H 6].[38] It inaugurated a long series of fountains that, in spite of their diverse forms and dimensions, were to perpetuate this Mamluk influence without a break until about 1750. The Sabīl of ʿAbdarraḥmān Katḫudā (1744), despite the originality of its decoration, is still described as "an elegant Mamluk pastiche" by M. Rogers [C. G 6].[39] We have already had the opportunity of noting that this faithfulness to Mamluk models was just as appreciable in domestic architecture, and in constructions for commercial use *(wakāla).*[40]

4. INNOVATION

This persistence of traditional architectural types, which, as more extensive studies will no doubt show, existed elsewhere than in Cairo, did not mean that there was a total stagnation in "national" forms while a small area was abandoned to imported "Ottoman" art. We noted previously that architects and craftsmen knew how to integrate elements taken from national repertories of forms and types

67. Sabīl of Ḫusrū Pasha in Cairo

of decoration into "Ottoman" monuments. In its development during the Ottoman era, the architecture of Arab cities, on the other hand, used elements drawn from Ottoman models and thereby enriched national art. At the same time, an internal evolution was making progress toward new forms in architecture and decoration.

The results of these interactions are sometimes of questionable quality, but the interest of an evolution toward a comparative fusion of elements taken from national tradition with imported elements is not to be denied.

4.1. Assimilation of Ottoman Elements

The assimilation of Ottoman elements is nowhere as apparent as in the fairly widespread adoption of the Ottoman minaret: its propagation finally gave the panoramas of Arab towns one of their most characteristic aspects.[41] One would certainly like to know the aesthetic and cultural reasons for this success. It is striking to notice that, of the four mosques of Cairo of typically Mamluk inspiration mentioned earlier, two have Ottoman minarets (Maḥmūd Pasha, ᶜUṯmān Katḫudā). The phenomenon is so widespread in Cairo that, instead of giving numerous examples, it would be simple to mention the exceptions, of which the Mosque of Muḥammad Bey (1774) is the most noteworthy.

The second area in which national architecture borrowed from the Ottoman repertory is that of decoration, particularly with the use of ceramics that were either directly imported or manufactured locally in imitation of Turkish production. Here again, it would be tedious to give examples. I will merely mention Tunis, where outside influences combined with very rich local traditions. Native craftsmanship was able to supply the products that fashion imposed: see the Hall of the Sulaymāniyya Madrasa (1754), as regards religious edifices [T. K 7]; and, among the countless examples in domestic architecture, the Dār ᶜUṯmān Dey (before 1611) and the Dār Ḥusayn (end of the eighteenth century). One could also mention Qayrawan with the amazing decoration of the Mosque "of the Barber" (seventeenth century). In Cairo ceramic decoration was abundantly used in the *sabīl* in small panels, on the facades, or, more extensively, on the walls of the water distribution rooms (as in the Sabīl of Muḥammad Katḫudā, no. 230, 1677). But the most famous example is that of the Mosque of Aq Sunqur (1347) where, on the occasion of important restoration work by Ibrāhīm Agha in 1652, the wall of the *qibla* was entirely covered with tiles of second-rate quality from Da-

68. Hall of the Sulaymāniyya Madrasa in Tunis

mascus, the tomb of the restorer being embellished with more refined decoration [C. P 5].[42]

4.2. Development of a Decorative Style

The Ottoman era saw the development of a more ornate, sometimes even excessive, decorative style that owed much to the very

69. Dār Ḥusayn in Tunis

varied influences received from Istanbul, but also from Europe and from Italy in particular, where the Arab countries bought large quantities of decorative elements: glassware, wood, marble. These influences constituted a baroque (or Levantine) decoration that took various aspects in different regions of the Arab world. One need only mention, for example, the stone decorative elements that had such a success in Aleppo as early as the seventeenth century (Bayt Ġazzāla, Bayt Ağīqbāš), or the definitely baroque decor of the Mosque "of the Barber" in Qayrawan. This tendency to an overornamentation appears in Cairo in neo-Mamluk *miḥrāb* of sometimes question-

70. *Qibla* wall of the Aq Sunqur Mosque in Cairo

able taste due to the rather poor quality of the materials used and clumsy execution, as in the *qibla* wall of the al-Burdaynī Mosque, with its rather crude execution,[43] or that of the Altī Barmaq Mosque (1711), which is truly barbarian. On facades this development resulted in the exuberance of the Sabīl of ʿAlī Bey al-Dimiyāṭī (1710), which was later imitated. But there were also more satisfactory results, in the detail of the adornment of the facade of the Yūsuf Čurbağī Mosque (1763), for example, where decorative balance is achieved with Mamluk elements, or again in some of the edifices built by ʿAb-

71. Sabīl of ʿAlī Bey al-Dimiyāṭī in Cairo

darraḥmān Katḫudā: the *zāwiya* (no. 214, c. 1754?), the al-Šawā-zliyya Mosque (no. 450, 1754), and above all the two *sabīl-maktab* (public fountain and school) of the al-Muṭahhar Mosque (no. 40, 1744) and of Naḥḥāsīn Street (no. 21, 1744). In this last monument, the Mamluk pastiche is just a background element for the development of a decoration that was very original in Cairo at that time and that in detail seems of Ottoman origin. The combination of these elements gives its originality to a monument that is unquestionably one of the great architectural achievements of Cairo, and not only for the Ottoman period.[44]

72. Sabīl of ʿAbdarraḥmān Katḫudā in Cairo (no. 21)

4.3. Innovation in Tunis and Cairo

Innovation in the architectural domain during the Ottoman era was not, however, restricted to decorative elements. Of the really new types of construction that appeared at that time we shall give two examples, in Tunis and in Cairo, a choice more or less imposed upon us by the present state of our information.

4.3.1. The appearance of a new type of funerary mosque in

73. Mosque and Turba of Yūsuf Dey in Tunis

Tunis undoubtedly bears some relation to the cosmopolitan character of Tunisia in the seventeenth century. The numerous ethnic elements that made up the ruling class in the regency transmitted cultural influences that a more thorough study would undoubtedly enable one to trace in the art of the period. To the Ifriqiyyan (Hafsid) component there were added, in a few generations, influences brought from the East (by the Turks), from the West (by the Andalusians), and from the northern Mediterranean (by the converts, in particular of Italian origin). The addition of these elements inevitably resulted in an art that was both heterogeneous and original.

The Mosque and Turba (mausoleum) of Yūsuf Dey (1610–1637) was built in 1616 by an architect of Spanish origin (Ibn Ġālib). The prayer hall of this suspended mosque, with its eight rows of six columns and its larger central nave, has an unquestionably Maghribian character. The courtyard enveloping the prayer hall on three sides (with a gallery on the north side) seems to be a development of Hafsid monument plans: it combines the layout of the al-Ḥaliq Mosque (built in 1375) with that of the Bāb al-Aqwās Mosque (which dates from the beginning of the fifteenth century); it may also have been influenced by the spatial organization of imperial mosques. The minaret, with its square base and octagonal section, evokes Ottoman minarets, but the form of the lantern is original. The square mausoleum, covered by a pyramidal roof, with green tiles, calls to mind Andalusian architecture (e.g., the monuments of the Alhambra); its decoration is also reminiscent of that of the palace of ʿUṯmān Dey, a monument that was built a few years earlier [T. J 5].[45]

The Mosque of Ḥammūda Pasha, built in 1655, is a development of the Mosque of Yūsuf Dey in its different elements: a prayer

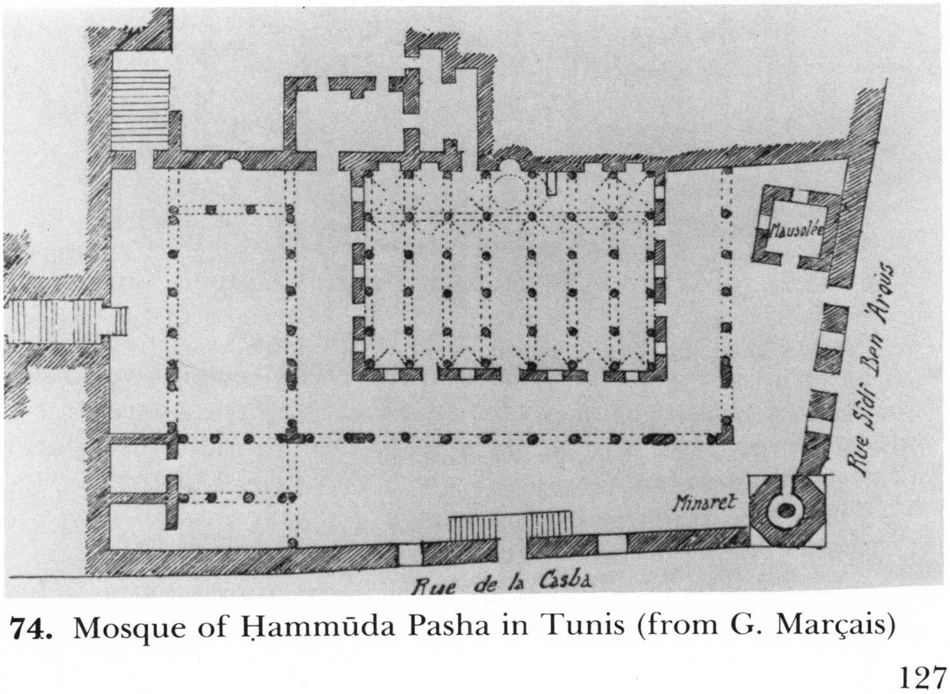

Mausolée
Rue Sidi Ben 'Arous
Minaret
Rue de la Casba

74. Mosque of Ḥammūda Pasha in Tunis (from G. Marçais)

75. Turba of Ḥammūda Pasha Mosque in Tunis

hall again in the "Maghribian" tradition, with seven naves instead of nine, five bays instead of seven; an enveloping courtyard, but with a gallery on three sides of the mosque; a minaret that, though notably elongated, is an obvious offspring of that of the Yūsuf Dey Mosque; a mausoleum similarly inspired by Yūsuf Dey's *turba,* with a decoration that displays some Italian features [T. I 6].[46]

These two very original and very harmonious monuments, despite the obviously composite character of their creation, had a lasting influence on Tunisian religious architecture. The enveloping portico of the Mosque of Ḥammūda Pasha is to be found around the Sidi Mehrez Mosque (1696) [T. B 5], which is a typically Ottoman monument, as we saw earlier; the octagonal minaret and lantern are reproduced exactly in the al-Ǧadīd Mosque of Ḥusayn bin ᶜAlī (1727). Finally, the Ṣāhib al-Ṭābiᶜ Mosque, built as late as 1814, is a more or less exact copy of the monuments of Yūsuf Dey and Ḥammūda Pasha, of which it embodies all the characteristics. The building is suspended; it has a "Maghribian" prayer hall (with nine naves) and an enveloping gallery.[47] The new type of mosque that appeared in Tunis at the beginning of the seventeenth century and that incorporated very diverse elements (local traditions, Andalusian and Ottoman influences, baroque reminiscences) into an original and attractive combination constituted, in its turn, a model that inspired later constructions.

4.3.2. A comparable development took place in Cairo after 1750, in the most typical monument of this town, the *sabīl*/fountains. For more than two centuries, the Cairo *sabīl* had followed Mamluk models. This tradition was interrupted, toward the middle of the eighteenth century, with the appearance of a new type of *sabīl* of round shape, the origins of which are perhaps to be found in the capital. From this point of view, and in the absence of more formal proof, it seems significant that the first example of a round *sabīl* in Cairo was precisely a foundation dedicated to a sultan. In 1750, Bašīr Agha Dār al-Saᶜāda built a fountain in the name of Sultan Maḥmūd, this monument being linked with a *takiyya* (convent), a typical Ottoman construction in Cairo [C. P 9].[48] The novelty of the plan (the facade of the fountain is semicircular with three windows surmounted by a polygonal *maktab),* the originality of decorative elements (columns, barred windows, floral elements), the canopies (the curves of which recall Istanbul roofs) are all the more striking, as this monument faces the wholly traditional *sabīl* erected there a few years earlier (no. 309, 1718).

This new type of *sabīl* was an obvious success in Cairo, as it was followed, during the second half of the eighteenth century, by the construction of similar monuments that are among the most interesting buildings of Cairo[49]: the Sabīl of Ibrāhīm Kathudā Mustaḥfiẓān (no. 331, 1753), badly damaged today (but Pascal Coste's fine sketches enable us to appreciate its original elegance: ornamental

76. Sultan Maḥmūd Fountain in Cairo (from P. Coste)

sculpted motifs with ceramic decoration); the Sabīl of Sultan Muṣṭafā, with its noteworthy polychromatic effects of the marbles on the facade (no. 314, 1759); the Sabīl of Ruqayya Dūdū (no. 337, 1760) [C. Q 6], the exuberant decoration of which achieves a sort of baroque climax; the Sabīl of Nafīsa al-Bayḍā, close to Bāb Zuwayla (no. 358, 1796); the Sabīl of the Ǧānbalāṭ Mosque, fine drawings of which are to be found in the *Description de l'Egypte* (no. 381, 1797); and last the Sabīl of Ḥusayn al-Šuʿaybī, which marked a sort of "banalization" of the round *sabīl* insofar as, in this case, the new form is incorporated into Mamluk architectural tradition (no. 588, end of the eighteenth century) [C. F 6].[50] This example of the *sabīl* shows that, despite the vigor of local tradition, Cairo architects were able to innovate; to develop new forms; and, finally, to make them part of the national repertory. This situation changed with the advent of the nineteenth century. Totally foreign forms were then purely and simply imported, and several Cairo *sabīl* of Muḥammad ʿAlī's period are but unimaginative pastiches of the Istanbul fountains.

77. Sabīl of Ruqayya Dūdū in Cairo

78. Sabīl of Ḥusayn al-Šuʿaybī in Cairo

5. CONCLUSION

Even in a field, that of art and culture, in which the balance of the Ottoman period is considered as being mainly negative, it is impossible to ignore the achievements of these four centuries of Arabo-Ottoman history. The indisputably unfortunate aspects of Ottoman domination and, above all, the disasters of the end of the nineteenth, and of the beginning of the twentieth, centuries must not make us underestimate a past that has deeply marked the evolution of the Arab cities.

A strong urban growth brought them to an unprecedented magnitude; and even if there were little originality in architectural creation, the Arab cities were the setting of an activity where impulses from the capital, local traditions, and numerous Mediterranean influences produced an original mixture.

It was during these four centuries of "modern" history that the Arab cities witnessed the progressive development, and the final completion, of the urban structures and decor that made up what can be termed the "traditional" Arab urban system. This maturation was completed at a time when the great mutations of the nineteenth century, and the irreversible mutilations of the twentieth, opened a new and completely different chapter in the millenary history of the Arab cities. For this reason alone it is important to look back to the Ottoman past of these cities.

Notes

1. In his book on the history of the Arabs, Dominique Sourdel devotes only one page (out of 128) to these four centuries of Ottoman history, and one sentence sums up the tone of his appraisal: "The Arab regions subject to Turkish rule knew both an economic and intellectual stagnation that was not to end before the 19th century." Dominique Sourdel, *Histoire des Arabes* (Paris, 1976), 105.

2. Marcel Colombe, *La vie au Caire au XVIIIe siècle* (Cairo, 1951), 1.

3. Edmond Pauty, "Etude sur les monuments de l'Egypte de la période ottomane," *Comité de Conservation* 37 (Cairo, 1933–1935), 295.

4. In his excellent book, *A History of Ottoman Architecture* (London, 1971), G. Goodwin gives for the ʿĀdiliyya of Aleppo (1555) the date of 1517, and he suggests for the Uṯmāniyya (1730) that of the sixteenth century (pp. 213 and 313).

5. From Edmond Pauty, *Les palais et les maisons d'époque musulmane au Caire* (Cairo, 1932), and *Les Hammams du Caire* (Cairo, 1933); especially see the article quoted in note 3 and his "L'Architecture au Caire depuis la conquête ottomane," *Bulletin de l'Institut Français d'Archéologie Orientale* 35 (1936–1937); L. Hautecoeur and Gaston Wiet, *Les mosquées du Caire,* 2 vols. (Paris, 1932).

6. J. A. Williams, "The Monuments of Ottoman Cairo," in André Raymond, M. Rogers and M. Wahba, eds., *Colloque international sur l'histoire du Caire* (D.D.R, n.d.), 453–463; M. Rogers, "Ḳāhira," in *Encyclopédie de l'Islam,* 2d ed. (Leiden-Paris, 1978), IV, 442–461.

7. See the very judicious remark of J. A. Williams, "The Monuments," 453.

8. These figures do not take into account the palaces and houses.

9. Classified with the number 128. See Max van Berchem, *Matériaux pour un corpus* (Cairo and Paris, 1894), 602–603; E. Prisse d'Avennes, *L'Art arabe* (Paris, 1877), 126–127, 272, 276; E. Pauty, "Architecture," 13–14 (plan); L. Hautecoeur and G. Wiet, *Mosquées,* I, 342–346; J. A. Williams, "The Monuments," 459; M. Rogers, "Ḳāhira," 455; G. Goodwin, *A History,* 312.

10. Jean Sauvaget, "Inventaire des monuments musulmans de la ville d'Alep," *Revue des Etudes Islamiques (REI)* (1931), no. 66, p. 99; G. Goodwin, *A History,* 202–203 (plan).

11. Kāmil al-Ġazzī, *Kitāb Nahr al-Ḏahab,* 3 vols. (Aleppo, 1342 H.), II, 111.

J. Sauvaget, "Inventaire," no. 63 (he gives the date of 1517, which is accepted by Goodwin).

12. H. Sauvaire, "Description de Damas," *Journal Asiatique* (1896), 253–281; M. Briggs, *Muhammadan Architecture* (Oxford, 1924), 136–137; Jean Sauvaget, *Les monuments historiques de Damas* (Beirut, 1932), no. 71, pp. 78–79; G. Goodwin, *A History*, 256–257, 291; A. Rihawi and E. Ouechek, "Les deux *Takiyya* de Damas" *Bulletin d'Etudes Orientales (BEO)* 28 (1975), 217–225 (plan).

13. A. Patricolo, "Compte rendu, "in *Comité de Conservation* 32 (1915–1919), 176–177 (plan); L. Hautecoeur and G. Wiet, *Mosquées,* 344–347; G. Goodwin, *A History,* 312; J. A. Williams, "The Monuments," 459; E. Pauty, "Architecture," 15.

14. H. Sauvaire,"Description," 260–261; J. Sauvaget, *Monuments,* no. 77, p. 83; Heinz Gaube, *Arabische Inschriften aus Syrien* (Beirut, 1978), 77, 81, 82.

15. K. Ġazzī, *Nahr,* II, 52; Albert Gabriel, "Les mosquées de Constantinople," *Syria* (1926), 371; J. Sauvaget, "Inventaire," no. 65.

16. J. Sauvaget, *Monuments,* no. 79, p. 86; H. Sauvaire, "Description," 262; H. Gaube, *Arabische Inschriften,* 89; G. Goodwin, *A History,* 300; Jean-Paul Pascual, *Damas à la fin du XVIe siècle* (Damascus, 1983), 33–34, 97–99.

17. Van Berchem, *Matériaux,* 610; A. Patricolo, "Compte rendu," 177–178, 180–181 (plan); M. Briggs, *Muhammadan Architecture,* 139–140; L. Hautecoeur and G. Wiet, *Mosquées,* 342–343; E. Pauty, "Architecture," 16–17; J. A. Williams, "The Monuments," 459; G. Goodwin, *A History,* 312; M. Rogers, "Ḳāhira," 455–456; Hadāya Taymūr, "Ǧāmi^{c} al-Malika Ṣafiya," thesis, University of Cairo, 1977.

18. A. Devoulx, *Les édifices religieux de l'ancien Alger* (Algiers, 1870), 132, 140, 142; G. Colin, *Corpus des inscriptions arabes et turques* (Paris, 1901), 46, 50–59; Georges Marçais, *L'Architecture musulmane d'Occident* (Paris, 1954), 433–434; Pierre Boyer, *La vie quotidienne à Alger à la veille de l'intervention française* (Paris, 1963), 74, 77; R. Dokali, *Les Mosquées de la période turque à Alger* (Algiers, 1974), 39–40 (plan).

19. G. Marçais, *L'Architecture,* 462–463; Slimane Mostafa Zbiss, *La Médina de Tunis* (Tunis, 1981), 20; G. Goodwin, *A History,* 358.

20. Rāġib al-Ṭabbāḫ, *I^{c}lām al-Nubalā,* 7 vols. (Aleppo, 1923–1926); K. Ġazzī, *Nahr,* II, 156–158; J. Sauvaget, "Inventaire," no. 73; A. Ṭalas, *al-Aṯār al-Islāmiyya fī Ḥalab* (Damascus, 1955), 136; J. Sauvaget, *Alep. Essai sur le développement d'une grande ville syrienne, des origines au milieu du XIXe siècle,* 2 vols. (Paris, 1941), Album, pl. LXVIII (plan); H. Gaube, *Arabische,* 22–23; G. Goodwin, *A History,* 313.

21. H. Gaube, *Arabische,* no. 155, p. 82 (with a wrong date: 1106/1695); Karl K. Barbir, *Ottoman Rule in Damascus* (Princeton, 1980), 86–88.

22. A. Patricolo, "Compte rendu," 182–185 (plan); E. Pauty, "L'Architecture," 15; L. Hautecoeur and G. Wiet, *Mosquées,* 344, 347; J. A. Williams, "The Monuments," 459.

23. Pascal Coste made a drawing of this minaret in *Architecture arabe* (Paris, 1839), pl. xxxvii.

24. J. A. Williams, "The Monuments," 454, 458.

25. J. A. Williams, "The Monuments," 458.

26. See Abdul-Karim Rafeq, *The Province of Damascus. 1723–1783* (Beirut, 1966), 276, and Daniel Crecelius, *The Roots of Modern Egypt* (Chicago, 1981), 145–147.

27. M. Rogers, "Ḳāhira," 455, 458; J. A. Williams, "The Monuments," 454.

28. J. A. Williams, "The Monuments," 458; M. Rogers, "Ḳāhira," 455.

29. L. Hautecoeur and G. Wiet, *Mosquées,* 351; E. Pauty, "L'Architecture," 3; J. A. Williams, "The Monuments," 454.

30. M. Rogers, "Ḳāhira," 456.

31. Classified with the number 135. Max Herz, "Appendice," in *Comité de Conservation* 23 (1906), 111, 120; L. Hautecoeur and G. Wiet, *Mosquées,* 344; E. Pauty, "Architecture," 12; J. A. Williams, "The Monuments," 456; M. Rogers, "Ḳāhira," 456.

32. Monument number 201. E. Prisse d'Avennes, *Art arabe,* 128–129, 267–268 (plan); van Berchem, *Matériaux,* 612–613; M. Briggs, *Muhammadan Architecture,* 143–144; L. Hautecoeur and G. Wiet, *Mosquées,* 341, 346; E. Pauty, "L'Architecture," 11.

33. Monument number 264. L. Hautecoeur and G. Wiet, *Mosquées,* I, 341; J. A. Williams, "The Monuments," 460.

34. André Raymond, "Les constructions de l'Emir ʿAbd al-Raḥmān Katḫudā au Caire," *Annales Islamologiques* 11 (1972).

35. Monument number 259. A. F. Mehren, "Description des Monuments du Caire," ms. (1869), 88–90; L. Hautecoeur and G. Wiet, *Mosquées,* 341; E. Pauty, "Architecture," 11.

36. Monument number 30. ʿAlī Pacha Mubārak, *al-Ḫiṭaṭ al-Ǧadīda,* 20 vols. (Būlāq, 1888), II, 74; V, 110; L. Hautecoeur and G. Wiet, *Mosquées,* 344–345.

37. E. Pauty, "Architecture," 22.

38. Monument number 52. Max Herz, *Comité de Conservation* 19 (1902), 142, 144; M. Rogers, "Ḳāhira," 455; André Raymond, "Les fontaines publiques *(sabīl)* du Caire," *Annales Islamologiques* 15 (1979).

39. Monument number 21. M. Rogers, "Ḳāhira," 455; A. Raymond, "Les fontaines publiques," no. 85, p. 271.

40. J. A. Williams, "The Monuments," 457.

41. See J. A. Williams, "The Monuments," 456–457.

42. J. A. Williams, "The Monuments," 457.

43. M. Rogers, "Ḳāhira," 456.

44. M. Rogers, "Ḳāhira," 455.

45. G. Marçais, *L'Architecture,* 459–462 (plan); S. M. Zbiss, *Médina,* 19, 29, and "Portes, baies et façades datées de Tunis," *Cahiers des Arts et Techniques de l'Afrique du Nord* 6 (1960), 148; J. Revault, *Palais,* I, 93–117.

46. G. Marçais, *L'Architecture,* 462–463 (plan); S. M. Zbiss, *Médina,* 20–29, and "Portes," 148.

47. G. Marçais, *L'Architecture,* 464 (plan).

48. Monument number 308. A. F. Mehren, "Description," 56; van Berchem, *Matériaux,* 624; A. Raymond, "Les fontaines publiques," no. 90, p. 273.

49. A total of seven *sabīl* in the new style out of 33 *sabīl* built between 1750 and 1798.

50. See A. Raymond, "Les fontaines publiques," no. 94, p. 275; no. 103, p. 279; no. 105, p. 279; no. 118, p. 284; no. 119, p. 284; no. 120, p. 284.

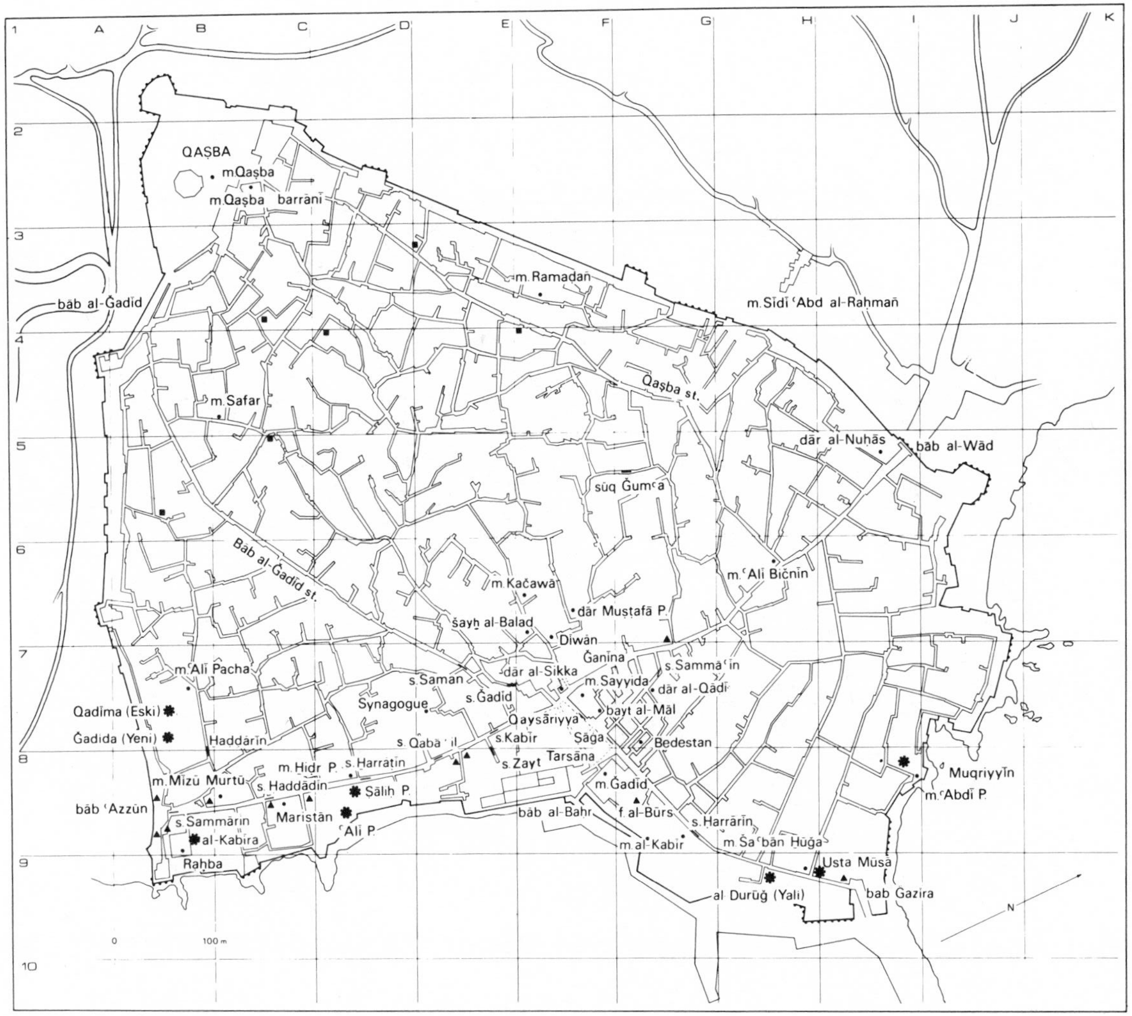

A
B
C
D
E
F
G
H
I
J
K
1
2
3
4
5
6
7
8
9
10
QAṢBA
m.Qaṣba
m.Qaṣba barrānī
bāb al-Ǧadīd
m.Ramaḍān
m.Sīdī ʿAbd al-Raḥman
m.Safar
Qaṣba st.
dār al-Nuḥās
bāb al-Wād
sūq Ǧumʿa
Bāb al-Ǧadīd st.
m.Kačawā
m.ʿAlī Bičnīn
dār Muṣṭafā P.
šayḫ al-Balad
Dīwān
Ǧanīna
dār al-Sikka
s.Sammāʿīn
m.Sayyida
dār al-Qāḍī
m.ʿAlī Pacha
s.Saman
s.Ǧadīd
Synagogue
bayt al-Māl
Qaysāriyya
Qadīma (Eski)
Ǧadīda (Yeni)
Haddārīn
s.Qabāʾil
s.Kabīr
Ṣāġa
Bedestan
s.Zayt
Tarsāna
m.Ḫiḍr P.
s.Harrātīn
m.Mizū Murtū
s.Haddādīn
Ṣāliḥ P.
m.Ǧadīd
Muqriyyīn
m.ʿAbdī P.
bāb ʿAzzūn
s.Sammārīn
al-Kabīra
Māristān
ʿAlī P.
bāb al-Baḥr
f. al-Būrš
s.Harrārīn
m.al-Kabīr
m.Šaʿbān Ḫūǧa
Raḥba
Usta Mūsā
al Durūǧ (Yalī)
bab Gazira
N
0
100 m

79. Plan of Algiers

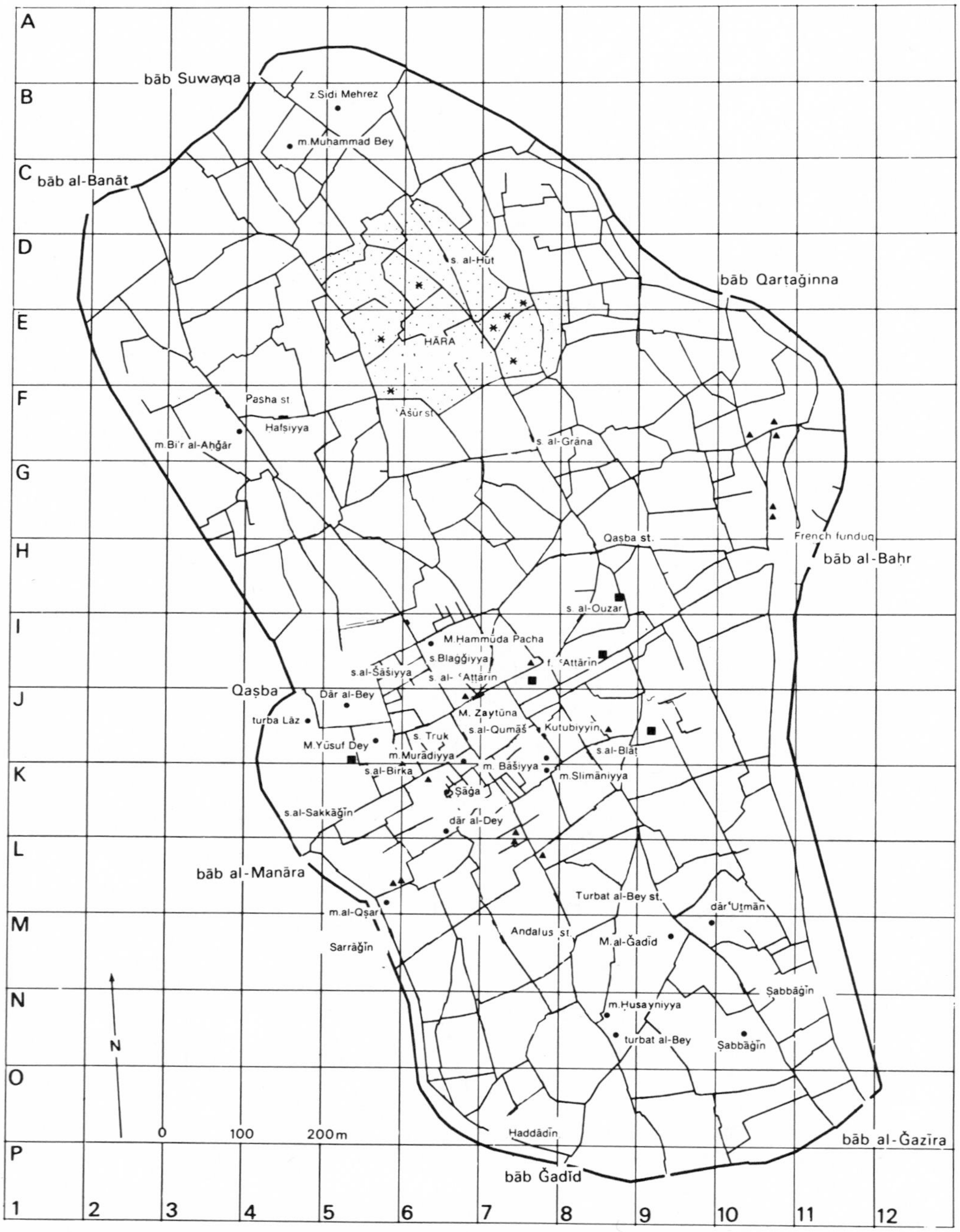
A
B
C
D
E
F
G
H
I
J
K
L
M
N
O
P
1
2
3
4
5
6
7
8
9
10
11
12
bāb Suwayqa
z.Sidi Mehrez
m.Muhammad Bey
bāb al-Banāt
s. al-Hūt
bāb Qartağinna
HĀRA
Pasha st.
Hafsiyya
m.Bi'r al-Aḥğār
'Āšūr st.
s. al-Grāna
Qaṣba st.
French funduq
bāb al-Bahr
s. al-Ouzar
M.Hammūda Pacha
s.Blagğiyya
f. 'Attārīn
s.al-Šāšiyya
s. al- 'Attārīn
Qaṣba
Dār al-Bey
M. Zaytūna
turba Lāz
s. Truk
s.al-Qumāš
Kutubiyyīn
M.Yūsuf Dey
m.Murādiyya
s.al-Blāt
m. Bāšiyya
s.al-Birka
m.Slimāniyya
Ṣāġa
s.al-Sakkāğīn
dār al-Dey
bāb al-Manāra
Turbat al-Bey st.
dār 'Uṯmān
m.al-Qṣar
Andalus st.
M.al-Ğadīd
Sarrāğīn
Ṣabbāğīn
m.Husayniyya
turbat al-Bey
Ṣabbāğīn
N
0
100
200m
Haddādīn
bāb al-Ğazīra
bāb Ğadīd

80. Plan of Tunis

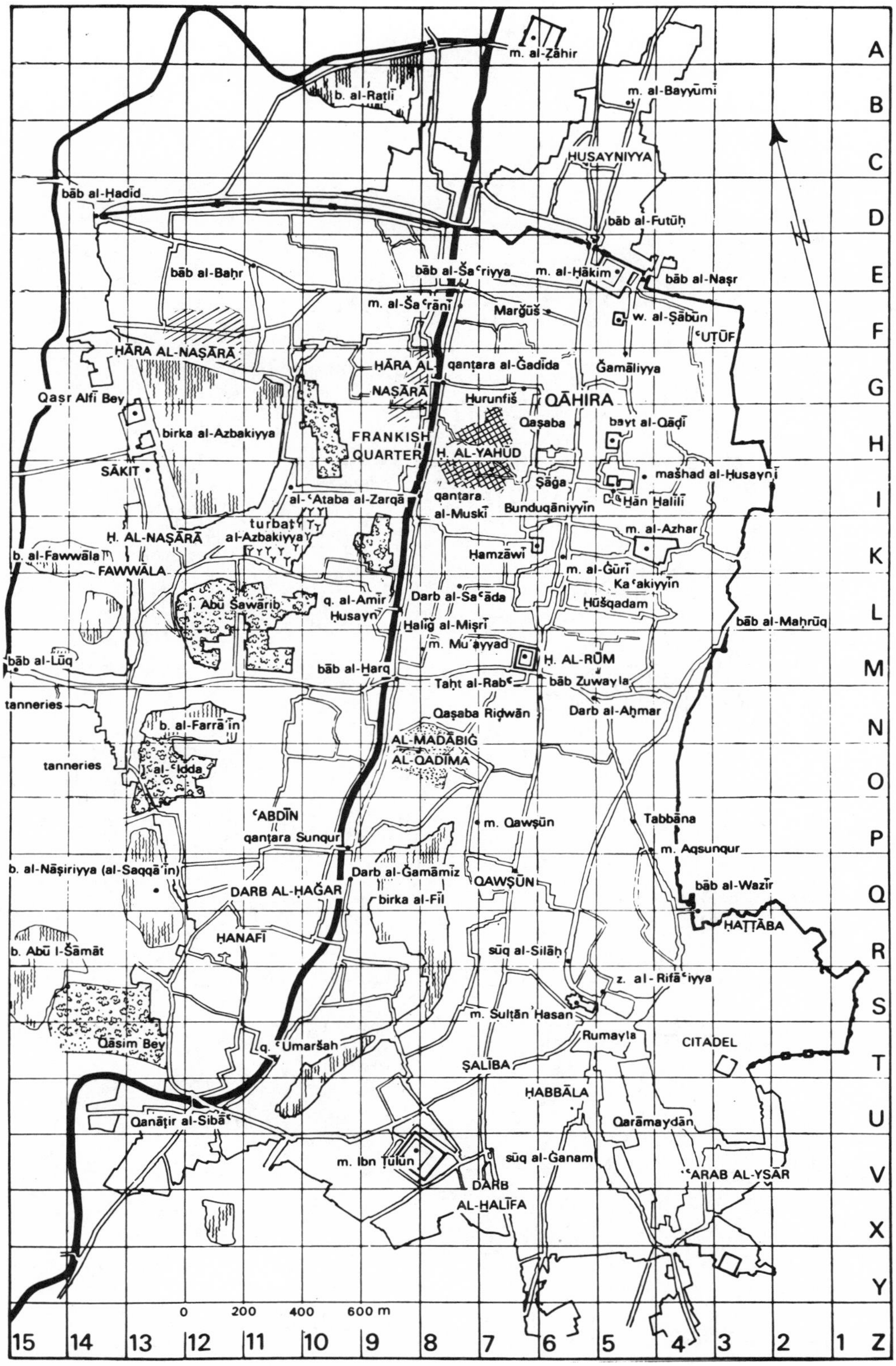
m. al-Ẓāhir
b. al-Raṭlī
m. al-Bayyūmī
ḤUSAYNIYYA
bāb al-Ḥadīd
bāb al-Futūḥ
bāb al-Baḥr
bāb al-Šaᶜriyya
m. al-Ḥākim
bāb al-Naṣr
m. al-Šaᶜrānī
Marǧūš
w. al-Ṣābūn
ᶜUṬŪF
ḤĀRA AL-NAṢĀRĀ
ḤĀRA AL-NAṢĀRĀ
qanṭara al-Ǧadīda
Ǧamāliyya
Qaṣr Alfī Bey
Ḫurunfiš
QĀHIRA
Qaṣaba
bayt al-Qāḍī
birka al-Azbakiyya
FRANKISH QUARTER
Ḥ. AL-YAHŪD
SĀKIT
Ṣāġa
mašhad al-Ḥusaynī
al-ᶜAtaba al-Zarqā
qanṭara al-Muskī
Bunduqāniyyīn
Ḫān Ḫalīlī
turbat al-Azbakiyya
Ḥ. AL-NAṢĀRĀ
m. al-Azhar
b. al-Fawwāla
FAWWĀLA
Ḥamzāwī
m. al-Ġūrī
Kaᶜakiyyīn
Abū Sawārib
q. al-Amīr Ḥusayn
Darb al-Saᶜāda
Ḫūšqadam
Ḫalīǧ al-Miṣrī
bāb al-Maḥrūq
m. Muᵓayyad
bāb al-Lūq
Ḥ. AL-RŪM
bāb al-Ḫarq
Taḥt al-Rabᶜ
bāb Zuwayla
tanneries
Qaṣaba Riḍwān
Darb al-Aḥmar
b. al-Farrāᵓin
AL-MADĀBIĠ AL-QADĪMA
tanneries
al-ᶜIdda
ᶜABDĪN
m. Qawṣūn
Tabbāna
qanṭara Sunqur
m. Aqsunqur
b. al-Nāṣiriyya (al-Saqqāᵓin)
Darb al-Ǧamāmīz
QAWṢŪN
bāb al-Wazīr
DARB AL-ḤAǦAR
birka al-Fīl
ḤAṬṬĀBA
ḤANAFĪ
b. Abū l-Šāmāt
sūq al-Silāḥ
z. al-Rifāᶜiyya
m. Sulṭān Ḥasan
Qāsim Bey
q. ᶜUmaršah
Rumayla
CITADEL
ṢALĪBA
ḤABBĀLA
Qanāṭir al-Sibāᶜ
Qarāmaydān
sūq al-Ġanam
m. Ibn Ṭūlūn
ᶜARAB AL-YSĀR
DARB AL-ḪALĪFA
0 200 400 600 m
A B C D E F G H I K L M N O P Q R S T U V X Y Z
15 14 13 12 11 10 9 8 7 6 5 4 3 2 1

81. Plan of Cairo

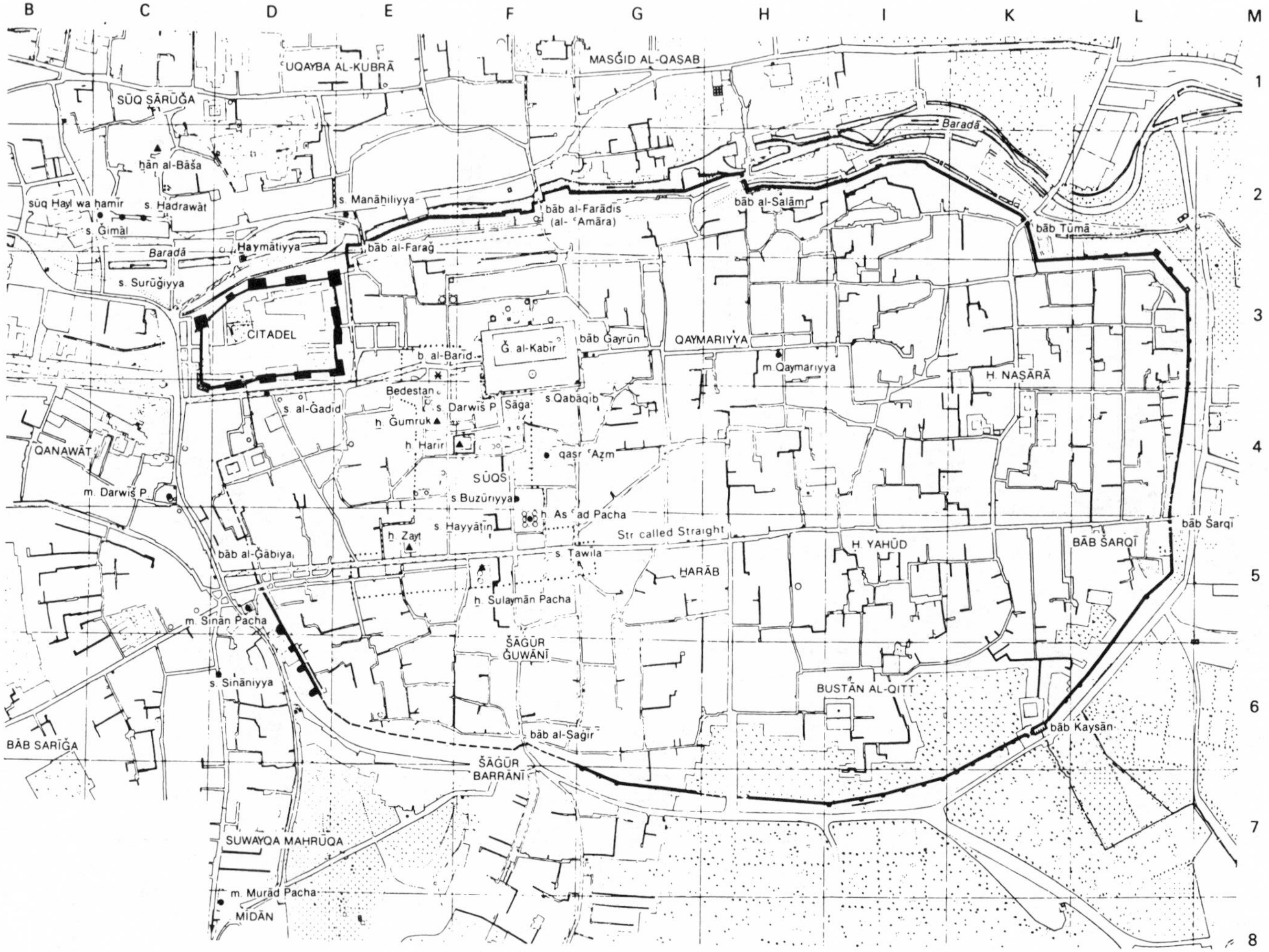

B
C
D
E
F
G
H
I
K
L
M
1
2
3
4
5
6
7
8
UQAYBA AL-KUBRĀ
MASĞID AL-QAṢAB
SŪQ ṢĀRŪĞA
ḫān al-Bāša
sūq Ḫayl wa ḥamīr
s. Ḥadrawāt
s. Ğimāl
Baradā
Haymātiyya
s. Surūğiyya
s. Manāḫiliyya
bāb al-Farādīs (al-ʿAmāra)
bāb al-Salām
Baradā
bāb Tūmā
bāb al-Farağ
CITADEL
Ğ. al-Kabīr
bāb Ğayrūn
QAYMARIYYA
m. Qaymariyya
H. NAṢĀRĀ
b. al-Barīd
Bedestan
s. Darwiš P.
Ṣāġa
s. Qabāqib
s. al-Ğadīd
ḫ. Ğumruk
ḫ. Ḥarīr
qaṣr ʿAẓm
QANAWĀT
SŪQS
m. Darwiš P.
s. Buzūriyya
ḫ. Asʿad Pacha
s. Ḫayyāṭīn
ḫ. Zayt
Str called Straight
bāb Šarqī
BĀB ŠARQĪ
H. YAHŪD
bāb al-Ğābiya
s. Ṭawīla
ḪARĀB
ḫ. Sulaymān Pacha
m. Sinān Pacha
ŠĀĠŪR ĠUWĀNĪ
s. Sināniyya
BUSTĀN AL-QIṬṬ
bāb Kaysān
BĀB SARĪĞA
bāb al-Ṣaġīr
ŠĀĠŪR BARRĀNĪ
SUWAYQA MAHRŪQA
m. Murād Pacha
MĪDĀN

82. Plan of Damascus

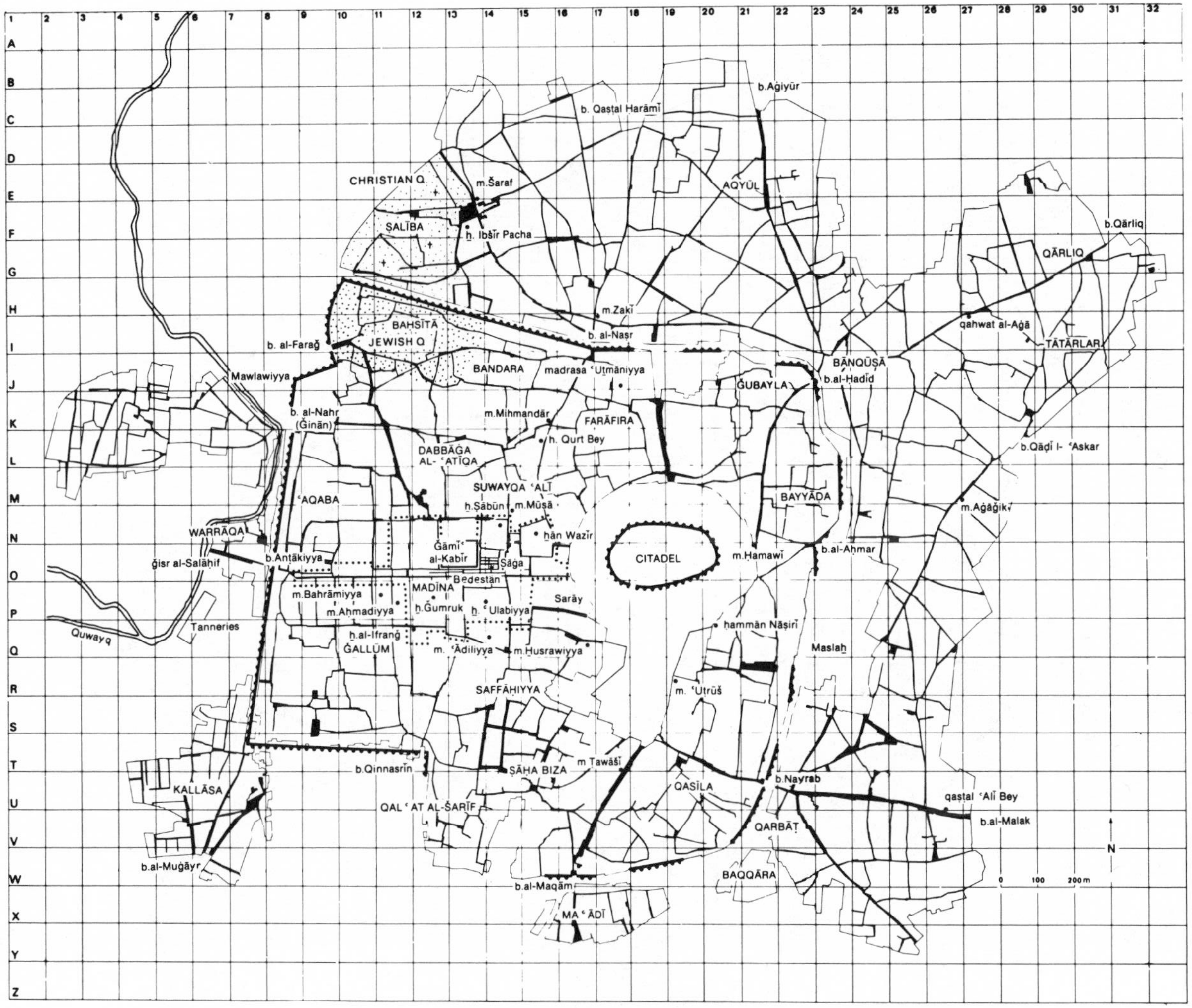
CITADEL
CHRISTIAN Q.
ṢALĪBA
BAHSĪTĀ
JEWISH Q.
BANDARA
DABBĀĠA AL-ʿATĪQA
ʿAQABA
WARRĀQA
MADĪNA
ĠALLŪM
SAFFĀHIYYA
ṢĀHA BIZA
QAL ʿAT AL-ŠARĪF
KALLĀSA
FARĀFIRA
SUWAYQA ʿALĪ
ĠUBAYLA
BAYYĀDA
BĀNQŪSĀ
AQYŪL
QĀRLIQ
TĀTĀRLAR
QASĪLA
QARBĀṬ
BAQQĀRA
MA ʿĀDĪ
Maslah
Sarāy
Tanneries
Quwayq
Mawlawiyya
b. al-Farağ
b. al-Nahr (Ğinān)
b. Antākiyya
ğisr al-Salāhif
b. Qinnasrīn
b. al-Muġāyr
b. al-Maqām
b. Nayrab
b. al-Ahmar
b. al-Hadīd
b. al-Naṣr
b. Qasṭal Harāmī
b. Aġiyūr
b. Qārliq
b. Qāḍī l- ʿAskar
b. al-Malak
qasṭal ʿAlī Bey
qahwat al-Aġā
m. Aġāğik
m. Ṣaraf
h. Ibšīr Pacha
m. Zakī
madrasa ʿUṯmāniyya
m. Mihmandār
h. Qurt Bey
h. Ṣābūn
m. Mūsā
hān Wazīr
Ğāmiʿ al-Kabīr
Ṣāġa
Bedestan
m. Bahrāmiyya
m. Ahmadiyya
h. Ğumruk
h. ʿUlabiyya
h. al-Ifranğ
m. ʿĀdiliyya
m. Husrawiyya
m. Hamawī
hammān Nāṣirī
m. ʿUtrūš
m Tawāšī
N
0 100 200 m

83. Plan of Aleppo

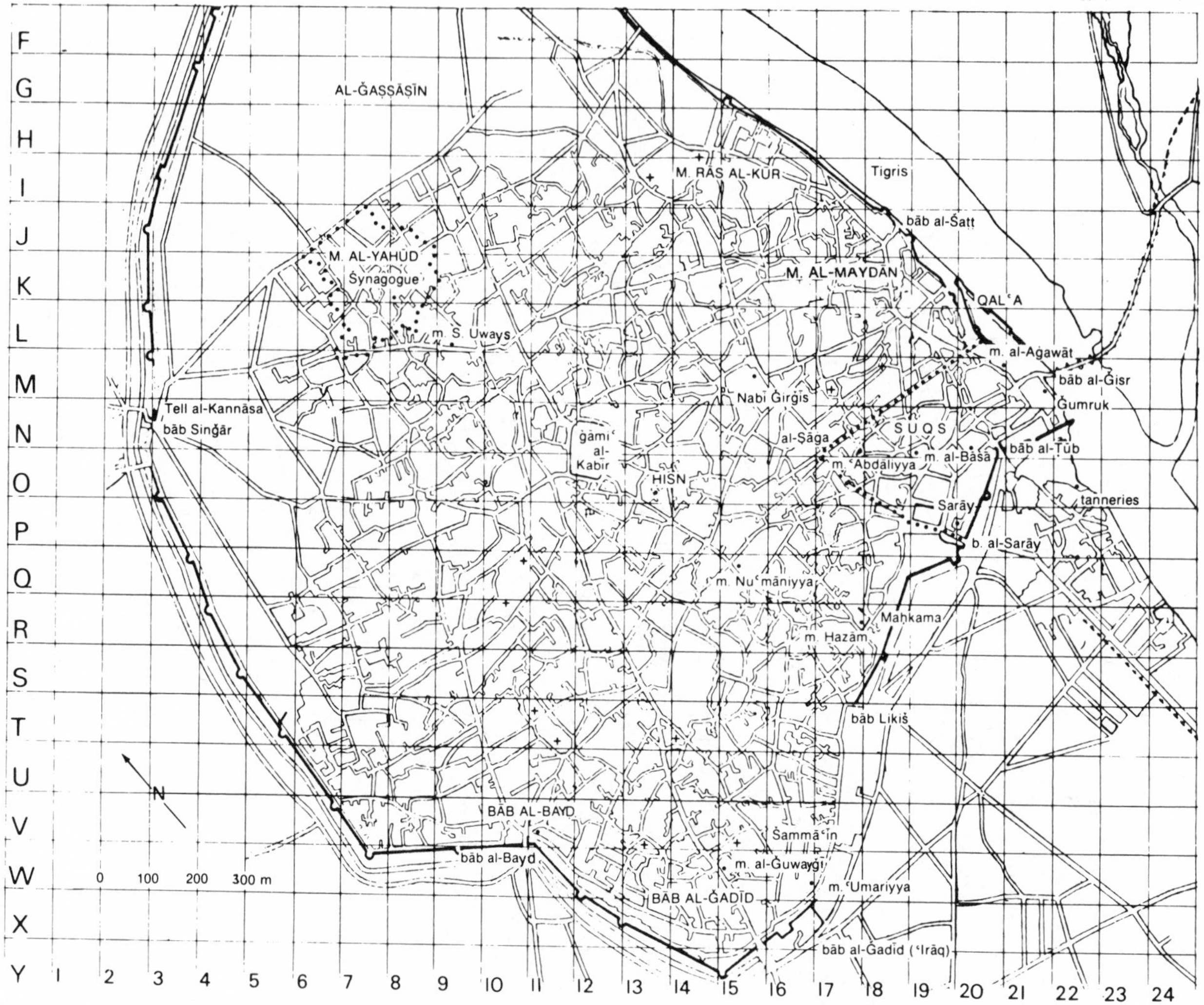
AL-ĠAṢṢĀṢĪN
M. RĀS AL-KŪR
Tigris
bāb al-Šaṭṭ
M. AL-YAHŪD
Synagogue
M. AL-MAYDĀN
QAL'A
m. S. Uways
m. al-Aġawāt
bāb al-Ġisr
Ġumruk
Tell al-Kannāsa
bāb Sinǧār
Nabī Ġirġis
SUQS
ǧāmi' al-Kabīr
al-Ṣāġa
bāb al-Ṭūb
m. 'Abdāliyya
m. al-Bāšā
HIṢN
Sarāy
tanneries
b. al-Sarāy
m. Nu'māniyya
Maḥkama
m. Hazām
bāb Likiš
N
BĀB AL-BAYḌ
Šammā'īn
bāb al-Bayḍ
m. al-Ġuwayǧī
0 100 200 300 m
m. 'Umariyya
BĀB AL-ǦADĪD
bāb al-Ǧadīd ('Irāq)
84. Plan of Mosul

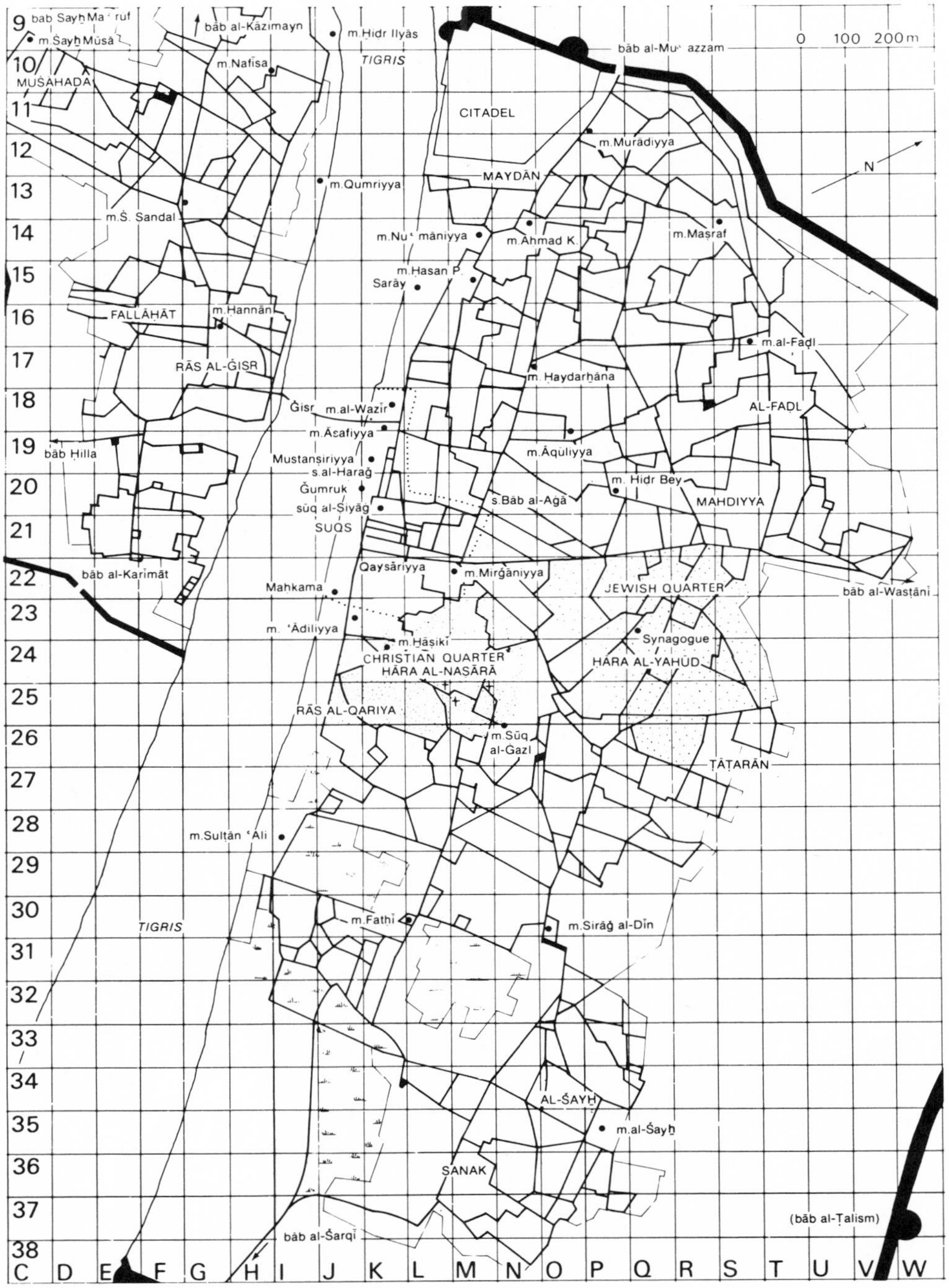
bab Sayḫ Ma'ruf
m. Sayḫ Mūsā
bāb al-Kāzimayn
m. Ḫiḍr Ilyās
TIGRIS
bāb al-Mu'azzam
0 100 200 m
m. Nafīsa
MUṢAHADA
CITADEL
m. Murādiyya
N
MAYDĀN
m. Qumriyya
m. Ṣ. Sandal
m. Nu'māniyya
m. Aḥmad K.
m. Maṣraf
m. Ḥasan P.
Sarāy
FALLĀḤĀT
m. Ḥannān
m. al-Faḍl
RĀS AL-ĠISR
m. Ḥaydarḫāna
Ġisr
m. al-Wazīr
m. Āṣafiyya
AL-FAḌL
bāb Ḥilla
m. Āqūliyya
Mustanṣiriyya
s. al-Harağ
Ğumruk
m. Ḫiḍr Bey
s. Bāb al-Aġā
MAHDIYYA
sūq al-Ṣiyāġ
SUQS
bāb al-Karīmāt
Qaysāriyya
m. Mirğāniyya
JEWISH QUARTER
bāb al-Wasṭānī
Maḥkama
m. 'Ādiliyya
m. Ḫāṣikī
Synagogue
CHRISTIAN QUARTER
ḤĀRA AL-NAṢĀRĀ
ḤĀRA AL-YAHŪD
RĀS AL-QARIYA
m. Sūq al-Ġazl
TĀTARĀN
m. Sulṭān 'Alī
TIGRIS
m. Fatḥī
m. Sirāğ al-Dīn
AL-ŠAYḪ
m. al-Šayḫ
SANAK
(bāb al-Ṭalism)
bāb al-Šarqī
9 10 11 12 13 14 15 16 17 18 19 20 21 22 23 24 25 26 27 28 29 30 31 32 33 34 35 36 37 38
C D E F G H I J K L M N O P Q R S T U V W

85. Plan of Baghdad

Selected Bibliography

Abdel Nour, Antoine. *Introduction à l'histoire urbaine de la Syrie ottomane (XVIe–XVIIIe siècle)*. Beirut, 1982.

Abu-Lughod, Janet L. *Cairo*. Princeton, 1971.

Bouhdiba, A., and Chevallier, D., eds. *La ville arabe dans l'Islam*. Tunis, 1982.

Boyer, Pierre. *La vie quotidienne à Alger à la veille de l'intervention française*. Paris, 1963.

Braude, B., and Lewis, B., eds. *Christians and Jews in the Ottoman Empire*. 2 vols. New York, 1982.

Brown, L. Carl, ed. *From Madina to Metropolis*. Princeton, 1973.

Brunschvig, Robert. "Urbanisme médiéval et droit musulman." *Revue des Etudes Islamiques* (1947): 127–155.

Caillé, J. *La ville de Rabat jusqu'au Protectorat français. Histoire et Archéologie*. 3 vols. Paris, 1949.

Chevallier, Dominique, ed. *L'Espace social de la ville arabe*. Paris, 1979.

Clerget, Marcel. *Le Caire*. 2 vols. Cairo, 1934.

Cohen, Amnon, and Lewis, Bernard. *Population and Revenue in the Towns of Palestine in the Sixteenth Century*. Princeton, 1978.

Daoulatli, Abdelaziz. *Tunis sous les Ḥafṣides*. Tunis, 1976.

Deverdun, Gaston. *Marrakech des origines à 1912*. 2 vols. Rabat, 1959.

Duri, A. A. "Baghdād." In *Encyclopédie de l'Islam*. 2d ed. Leyde-Paris, 1960. I, 921–936.

Elisséeff, Nikita. "Dimashḳ." In *Encyclopédie de l'Islam*. 2d ed. Leyde-Paris, 1965. II, 286–300.

Garcin, Jean-Claude. *Un centre musulman de la Haute-Egypte médiévale: Qūṣ*. Cairo, 1976.

Garcin, Jean-Claude; Maury, Bernard; Revault, Jacques; and Zakariya, Mona. *Palais et maisons du Caire, I, Epoque mamelouke.* Paris, 1982.

Gaube, Heinz. *Iranian Cities.* New York, 1979.

Gaube, Heinz, and Wirth, Eugen. *Der Bazar von Isfahan.* Wiesbaden, 1978.

Genabi, (al-), Hashim K. N. *Der Suq (Bazar) von Bagdad.* Erlangen, 1976.

Grabar, Oleg. "The Architecture of the Middle Eastern City from Past to Present: The Case of the Mosque." In *Middle Eastern Cities,* ed. I. Lapidus. Berkeley, 1969. 26–46.

Hourani, A. H., and Stern, S., eds. *The Islamic City.* Oxford, 1970.

Johansen, Baber. "The All-Embracing Town and Its Mosques." *Revue de l'Occident Musulman et de la Méditerranée* 32, no. 2 (1981).

Lane, Edward W. *Manners and Customs of the Modern Egyptians.* Rev. ed. London, 1954.

Lapidus, Ira M., ed. *Middle Eastern Cities.* Berkeley, 1969.

——. *Muslim Cities in the Later Middle Ages.* Cambridge, Mass., 1967.

Lespès, René. *Alger.* Paris, 1930.

Le Tourneau, Roger. *Fès avant le Protectorat.* Casablanca and Paris, 1949.

———. *Les villes musulmanes de l'Afrique du Nord.* Algiers, 1957.

Lézine, Alexandre. *Deux villes d'Ifriqiya.* Paris, 1971.

Mantran, Robert. *Istanbul dans la seconde moitié du XVIIe siècle.* Paris, 1962.

Marçais, Georges. "L'Urbanisme musulman." In *Mélanges d'histoire et d'archéologie de l'Occident musulman.* 2 vols. Algiers, 1957. I, 211–231.

Marçais, William. "L'Islamisme et la vie urbaine." In *Articles et conférences.* Paris, 1961.

Massignon, Louis. *Mission en Mésopotamie (1907–1908).* 2 vols. Cairo, 1912.

Maury, Bernard; Raymond, André; Revault, Jacques; and Zakariya, Mona. *Palais et maisons du Caire, II, Epoque ottomane.* Paris, 1983.

Rafeq, Abdul-Karim. *The Province of Damascus. 1723–1783.* Beirut, 1966.

Ra'ūf, ʿImād. *al-Mawṣil fī l-ʿahd al-ʿuṯmānī.* Al-Nağaf, Iraq, 1975.

Raymond, André. *Artisans et commerçants au Caire au XVIIIème siècle.* 2 vols. Damascus, 1974.

———. "Le Caire sous les Ottomans (1517–1798)." In Bernard Maury et al., *Palais et maisons du Caire, II, Epoque ottomane.* Paris, 1983.

Raymond, André; Rogers, M.; and Wahba, M., eds. *Colloque international sur l'histoire du Caire.* D.D.R., [1972].

Revault, Jacques. *Palais et demeures de Tunis.* 4 vols. Paris, 1967–1978.

Rogers, Michael. "Ḳāhira." In *Encyclopédie de l'Islam.* 2d ed. Leiden-Paris, 1978. IV, 442–461.

Sauvaget, Jean. *Alep. Essai sur le développement d'une grande ville syrienne, des origines au milieu du XIXe siècle.* 2 vols. Paris, 1941.

———. "Esquisse d'une histoire de la ville de Damas." *Revue des Etudes Islamiques* 4 (1934):421–480.

Serageldin, I., and El-Sadek, S., eds. *The Arab City. Its Character and Islamic Cultural Heritage.* N.p., 1982.

Serjeant, R. B., ed. *The Islamic City.* Paris, 1980.

Serjeant, R. B., and Lewcock, R. *Ṣanʿāʾ. An Arabian Islamic City.* London, 1983.

Shaw, Stanford J. *The Financial and Administrative Organization of Ottoman Egypt. 1517–1798.* Princeton, 1962.

Sims, Eleanor. "Trade and Travel: Markets and Caravanserais." In *Architecture of the Islamic World,* ed. G. Michell. New York, 1978.

Todorov, Nicolaj. *La ville balkanique aux XVe–XIXe siècles.* Bucharest, 1980.

Torres, Balbás, Leopoldo. *Ciudades Hispano-Musulmanas.* 2 vols. [Madrid], n.d.

———. "Les villes musulmanes d'Espagne et leur urbanisation." *Annales de l'Institut d'Etudes Orientales* 6 (1942–1947): 5–30.

Wiet, Gaston. *Cairo, City of Art and Commerce.* Norman, Okla., 1964.

Wirth, Eugen. "Die orientalische Stadt." *Saeculum* 26, 1 (1975): 45–94.

———. "Villes islamiques, villes arabes, villes orientales? Une problématique face au changement." In *La ville arabe dans l'Islam,* eds. A. Bouhdiba and D. Chevallier. Tunis, 1982. 193–225.

———. "Zum Problem des Bazars (suq, çarşi)." *Der Islam* 51 (1974): 203–260; 52 (1975): 6–46.

Index

The references concerning one particular city are given after the mention of its name. The names of the cities are arranged in alphabetical order. Page numbers in italics indicate illustrations.

Bāb Suwayqa (suburb of Tunis), 19, 33, 61